BACK........'S KITCHEN

Penny Paterson works in marketing communications, but her true passions are cooking and travel. She has travelled throughout the United Kingdom, Europe, South America, Australia and Asia and is currently planning a trip through Africa.

Caroline Paterson is an experienced and passionate cook, who enjoys creating anything from a humble family pasta dish to a five course dinner party. She was in her late teens when she first ventured overseas and has continued travelling extensively with her husband ever since.

This mother and daughter team's combination of travel experience and love of good food will make this an educational and interesting approach to cooking budget meals.

THE
BACKPACKER'S
KITCHEN

Penny and Caroline Paterson

Robert Hale • London

© Penny and Caroline Paterson 2010
First published in Great Britain 2010

ISBN 978-0-7090-8952-0

Robert Hale Limited
Clerkenwell House
Clerkenwell Green
London EC1R 0HT

www.halebooks.com

The right of Penny and Caroline Paterson to be identified
as authors of this work has been asserted by them
in accordance with the Copyright, Designs and
Patents Act 1988

A catalogue record for this book is available from the British Library

2 4 6 8 10 9 7 5 3 1

Illustrations by Yvonne Hacon

Design by Eurodesign

Printed in China

Contents

Cooking Whilst Backpacking: All You Need to Know 7

Food from Around the World 13

Snacks and Soups 23

Chicken Dishes 39

Meat Dishes 56

Fish Dishes 75

Pasta and Rice Dishes 87

Vegetarian Dishes 106

Vegetables and Salads 117

Desserts 131

Glossary 142

Conversions 144

Recipe Index 148

Cooking Whilst Backpacking: All You Need to Know

When you're about to head off travelling, the last thing you're probably thinking about is how experienced you are in a kitchen. Yes, you may have made the odd meal at home or heated up some baked beans or pizza, but not many of us carry around an array of recipes in our head.

That's where we come in! We've designed this book to ensure that you can always lay your hands on a range of healthy, interesting and delicious recipes, so that you can concentrate on more important things – like where you're going to sleep.

Why this book is an essential travel companion

Enjoying a country's cuisine is one of the highlights of any travel experience. Even though some destinations are world renowned for their food and local produce, eating in restaurants every night will put a great deal of strain on the average backpacker's budget. Most of us would never consider dining out every night at home, so why would we expect to while travelling?

There is a way to make the most of local ingredients and keep the costs down – by cooking yourself. Most hostels now offer kitchens equipped with a range of cooking facilities that you can use free of charge. These facilities vary considerably from location to location, so don't be surprised to find a restaurant-quality kitchen one day and a basic stove the next.

By cooking your own meals you will also be able to experience vibrant local markets. Often considered the social heart of any town, markets offer a range of fresh produce as well as pre-prepared delicacies that are perfect for snacking. You can also interact with some colourful local characters including native growers and farmers.

Also, the kitchen is often the only communal area of a hostel and so becomes the social hub. It is a great place to meet other back-packers and swap travel stories, especially if you are travelling alone.

To start you off, we've included some basic cooking advice at the beginning of most sections. We know that you may not have had a great deal of experience in a kitchen, so hope this will help you gain confidence cooking things like meat and rice and enable you to make your own dishes in addition to those in this book.

However, we appreciate that you will want to go out and experi-ence the local cuisine first hand, so have developed an overview of the different dishes you may come across while you are on your travels. The Food from Around the World section is designed to provide you with a taste of things to expect, and perhaps inspire you to try something a bit different.

We hope you get plenty of use and lots of enjoyment out of this book. We've aimed to make the recipes as simple to follow as possible, whilst maximizing the use of local produce.

Keep in mind:
- This book is not meant to replace dining out entirely. It's meant to provide some relief to your budget so you can enjoy your meals out guilt-free.
- You'll need to be flexible when it comes to the availability and quality of ingredients. Substitution will be key.
- Be inspired by the locals! If you see something on a restaurant menu that looks interesting, make note of the ingredients and try to re-create it back at the hostel.

- Recipes in this book may not be exactly the same as those you make at home. That's because we've tried to make them simple, including as few ingredients and cooking processes as possible. We've also tried to make sure that all the ingredients will be accessible during your travels, so have not included things like flour, which would be impractical to carry around in your backpack. Think of these recipes as the cheat version of your home-cooked favourites!
- All of the recipes are made for two! Cooking for one is always tricky, and we figured that you could maximize the cost of your ingredients by eating leftovers the next day, or sharing your food with your travel buddy or new-found friends.

What to expect from a hostel kitchen

Most hostels across the world are now recognizing the need to provide travellers with a self-catering option. However, the quality and variety of cooking facilities will vary significantly and the cost of the hostel per night will probably reflect this.

If you plan to do a fair amount of cooking on the road, it's worth enquiring about kitchen facilities when you book your accommodation. This will not only help you plan your budget more effectively, but also allow you to buy ingredients on the way to the hostel, knowing what facilities you will have available.

Newer hostels often have kitchens purpose-built for large groups and offer a variety of cooking stations (oven, stove, microwave) as well as every utensil, pot and pan you could hope for. Many, however, only have one cooking option (most commonly a stove), a mismatched saucepan and frying pan, and the odd knife or spatula. Some hostels have very poor facilities.

You may find a small range of ingredients in the hostel kitchen, such as olive oil, salt, pepper, herbs and garlic. These are sometimes supplied by the hostel, but most often have been left by previous travellers who have not been able to take the food with them. Feel free to use these because at some point along the way, you'll probably be leaving behind food of your own.

What to bring from home

As outlined in the previous chapter, most hostels will supply you with the basic facilities needed to cook the recipes in this book. However, it is also useful to bring a few bits and pieces from home which will make life easier for you while cooking on the road.

Utensils:
- A small sharp knife
- A teaspoon and tablespoon
- A few small re-sealable plastic bags

We've tried to keep the number of dried herbs and spices in the book to a minimum so that you don't have to carry much around with you. We've also included a range of fresh herbs that you should be able to access easily from markets and shops while travelling.

Flavourings:
- Curry powder
- Dried Italian herbs
- Chicken stock cubes. When using stock cubes allow 1 for every cup of boiling water.

General hygiene and safety advice

It is important to note that you can get food poisoning from meat and chicken that are not stored, prepared and cooked properly.

Therefore you should always follow these golden rules:

- Wrap raw meat/chicken in cling film or place in a sealed container when storing in the refrigerator so it doesn't contaminate other foods.
- Keep raw meat/chicken refrigerated until you want to cook it.
- Use a separate chopping board and knife when preparing the meat/chicken and wash thoroughly before using again.
- Wash your hands before and after handling raw meat/chicken.
- Do not put the cooked meat/chicken back onto the chopping board you used to prepare it unless the board has been washed thoroughly.
- Do not put very hot meat/chicken in the refrigerator; wait until it cools down.

Substitutions

We have tried to keep in mind the accessibility of ingredients when developing these recipes; however, there will be times when you are unable to source a particular ingredient. On these occasions, just try to think of another ingredient that has a similar flavour and texture to the one you need.

Here are a few ideas:

- It is easy to swap vegetables as long as they belong in the same 'family' (see page 118).
- When using dried herbs instead of fresh herbs, remember that the dried version has a much stronger flavour, so you only need to use half the quantity.
- Lemon and lime can be exchanged, but lime juice is a little stronger-tasting.
- Parmesan, pecorino and romano cheeses are interchangeable.
- You can use butter instead of oil when pan frying food, but it will burn easily if you're cooking over a high heat.

Food from Around the World

This section of the book is designed to provide you with some basic information about local specialties and ingredients you may come across during your travels.

While you may wish to be ambitious and try to create your own version of the dishes in the hostel kitchen, it might be easier to treat yourself with a meal out!

Otherwise, make the most of the fresh local produce you find and try incorporating them into the recipes contained in this book.

Europe

UNITED KINGDOM AND IRELAND

British cuisine is sometimes criticized for being plain and simple, based around the concept of meat and three veg. However, some of the world's great classic dishes come from the UK including fish and chips, bangers and mash, and the traditional Sunday roast.

The pub culture in Great Britain has gone through a transition in the past ten years, and the humble watering hole has given way to the gastro-pub. There has also been a revival of traditional hot puddings, served with lashings of custard, which are a real treat for dessert lovers.

Each country has its own local delicacies to offer, including Scottish haggis, Welsh laverbread and, within England, you have regional specialties such as Lancashire hotpot, Yorkshire pudding and Cornish pasty. Of course, you must also have a cream tea with clotted cream. A traditional Irish stew is well worth trying, as is soda bread and the range of potato dishes available in Ireland, including champ, colcannon and boxty.

Make sure you indulge in the wide range of real ales available all across the UK, and have a Guinness or two while you're in Ireland. If you like something a bit stronger, Scotland and Ireland distil some of the world's best whiskey.

WESTERN EUROPE

German cuisine is a carnivore's dream, consisting of a vast array of roasted meats and sausages. These hearty dishes are usually accompanied by side servings of sauerkraut and potatoes. In neighbouring Austria be sure to try the famous veal and pork schnitzels.

While in Belgium, tuck into a plate of moules et frites, fresh mussels and chips served with mayonnaise. There is also a wide range of sweet treats available, including Belgian waffles and their world-renowned chocolate.

France is well known for the richness of its cuisine and quality of its wine. Visiting a fresh food market is a wonderful experience and you'll find it hard to resist the local patisserie or crêperie so don't try to watch your waistline while you're there. Enjoy specialties including coq au vin, escargot (snails), cassoulet and bouillabaisse if you get the opportunity.

When visiting Scandinavia, take advantage of the plentiful seafood available, either fresh, pickled or smoked. Make sure you experience the traditional buffet of multiple dishes commonly referred to as a smorgasbord.

For cheese lovers, there is a vast range to sample in this part of the world, including Camembert in France, Gouda in the Netherlands and Gruyère in Switzerland. If you have a sweet tooth, enjoy Sachertorte and strudels in Austria, Black Forest gateau in Germany and éclairs in France.

MEDITERRANEAN EUROPE

Many countries bordering the Mediterranean Sea, including Spain, Italy, Portugal and southern France, enjoy a diet based on ingredients such as olive oil, onions, garlic and tomatoes combined with a wide range of colourful vegetables, including aubergines/eggplants, peppers and mushrooms. Fish and seafood are prominent in many dishes, as are meats such as lamb, goat, pork and rabbit.

In Spain, you can enjoy tapas, which involves a number of small plates of hot and cold food shared amongst diners. Favourites include chorizo al vino (spicy sausage cooked in wine), patatas bravas (fried potatoes with tomato salsa) and tortilla espanola (potato omelette).

In Italy, the home of pizza and pasta, try starting your meal with antipasto, a range of local meats, such as prosciutto and salami, and cheeses, like pecorino or fontina, served with pickled vegetables.

Try souvlaki in Greece and, if you have a sweet tooth, you will love the sticky, flaky baklava or the cinnamon-coated doughnuts called loukoumades.

Many of these countries have their own liqueurs served either as an aperitif before the meal, or afterwards with coffee. Try pastis in France, limoncello in Italy and ouzo in Greece.

CENTRAL AND EASTERN EUROPE

Eastern European cuisine is rich and hearty, traditionally comprising goulashes, stews, soups and dumplings. You'll also find a range of cabbage dishes, heavy breads, pickled vegetables and fresh vegetable salads accompanying the main meals.

Russian borscht, a soup made of beetroots, is definitely worth a try and, if you like sausages, you'll be spoiled for choice in Hungary.

In Georgia, you will find a delicious cheese pie called khachapuri being sold on most street corners; this is basically bread or pastry dough stuffed with cheese.

In the Czech Republic you can enjoy both savoury and sweet pancakes – the latter served with hot stewed fruit, which you'll always find room for even after a heavy meal.

If you're looking to try some regional brews, Russia makes the world's best vodka and the Czech Republic produces top quality pilsner beers.

Africa

MIDDLE EAST AND NORTH AFRICA

Middle Eastern countries such as Egypt, Morocco, Lebanon and Turkey use a wide range of spices and aromatics including cumin, coriander, cinnamon, paprika, cayenne pepper and cardamom seeds. You'll also come across a distinctive new spice called sumac, which is made from crushed, dried sour berries.

Kebabs and falafel are probably the most well known dishes, and can be found throughout the region. Kebabs are available in a wide range of forms, from shish skewers, made from meat threaded with vegetables and grilled over hot coals, to doner kebabs, which are slices of lamb or beef cut from a vertical rotating spit. All come served in pita bread with salad and garlic or chilli sauces.

Falafel is made from spiced chickpeas that are usually shaped into balls and then deep fried. They make a great snack, either on their own or in pita bread with salad, and can be found on street corners everywhere.

Meze is a selection of small dishes, and comprises hummus, olives, cheeses, meats, pickled vegetables and pita bread. It is great as an appetizer or as a main meal, and will allow you to try a range of different local delicacies.

Tagines are popular in the North African countries of Morocco, Tunisia and Algeria. Meat stews are cooked in traditional clay pots comprising a round flat disc topped with a cone shaped lid. These dishes are usually accompanied by couscous, lentils, chickpeas or pita bread.

Turkish coffee is definitely worth a try, and will surprise you with its thick density and strong flavour. Try it with Turkish delight as a sweet treat. Mint tea is also served in a range of countries and will be ceremoniously poured into glasses from a great height in order to mix the leaves together.

REST OF AFRICA

You will find that the food in Africa varies significantly depending on where you are and what is readily available. Most countries, however, will subsist on plenty of whole grains and beans as well as fresh fruit and vegetables.

The most common ingredients include maize, millet, beans and vegetables like corn, cassava, plantain and yams.

Animals such as cattle, sheep and goats are often used as a symbol of wealth and not commonly included in the local diet. However, you will come across wild animals such as crocodile, monkey, antelope and warthog on some menus, as well as the usual beef, chicken and seafood.

In South Africa, make sure you try baboetie, a tasty casserole made from beef mince, mashed potatoes, apricots, raisins and almonds.

It's also worth sampling nyama choma, an East African barbeque, which usually comprises mutton, goat or pork.

Drinking-wise, South Africa is famous for its 'new world' wines and Kenya makes some of the best coffee in the world.

Asia

EASTERN ASIA

Many meals in Eastern Asian countries such as China and Taiwan consist of rice and noodles served with accompanying meat and vegetables. Pork and chicken are popular meats, and you'll also find a variety of seafood along the coastlines. Stir-frying is the most popular style of cooking, with ingredients cut into bitesize pieces and then eaten with chopsticks.

Most people will think they have tried Japanese food by sampling a nori roll at their local YO! Sushi, but Japanese food is much more exciting and complex than that. Japanese cooking, unlike its neighbours', does not use many spices and concentrates on the pure, clean flavours of its local ingredients, such as fish, seafood, soy and vegetables. One of the most popular dishes is ramen, a noodle dish topped with soup and a mix of meat and vegetables.

While in Hong Kong, sample traditional dim sum, a range of small dishes of vegetables, meats and seafood served on a little steamer basket or plate. A Korean barbecue is also worth trying, with pieces of beef, pork and chicken prepared and grilled at the diner's table on gas or charcoal. In Korea, be mindful when you see gaejang-guk on the menu because it is a stew-style soup made using dog meat.

INDIAN SUBCONTINENT

Curry always springs to mind when thinking about the food in countries such as India, Pakistan, Sri Lanka, Nepal and Bangladesh. However, the spices and flavours used in different regions vary significantly, as do the key ingredients.

For example, the Bangladeshi diet consists mainly of curries made from fish or mutton, with vegetables including potato, aubergine/eggplant and tomatoes. However, in Sri Lanka, locals eat fish, poultry, lentils, meat and game curries, and often include coconut milk in their recipes.

Different cooking methods are also used. For example, the tandoor is used in Indian cooking to create the famous tandoori chicken; this is made by marinating the meat in spices, then baking in a clay oven at extremely high temperatures.

Curries are often served with rice and different types of bread, such as naan or chapatti, depending where you are. You will also find a wide range of condiments available including chutneys and sambals, which are made from coconut, onions, lime juice and chillies, and are generally very spicy.

It's important to know that cows are considered sacred in the Hindu religion, so you will be hard pressed to find beef in that part of the world. If you're feeling adventurous, you could try buffalo instead.

While in India, indulge in a lassi, which is a yogurt-based drink, mixed with spices. You can get sweet or savoury versions that are the perfect pick-me-up on a hot day!

CENTRAL ASIA

Central Asian cuisine reflects its nomadic roots, where people traditionally live on the meat and products of their herds. Therefore, you'll find their diet staples include mutton, goat and horse, as well as plenty of dairy products such as cheese, yogurt and milk.

Most meals are served as stews, usually accompanied by dumplings. You'll also find kebabs, also known as shaslik, in many countries, which consist of skewered pieces of meat cooked over hot coals and served with flat bread.

You will be able to find plenty of fresh fruit, dried fruit and nuts at the local markets, which may keep you sustained if you tire of gambling with unidentifiable meats.

Remember when eating with locals and there is no cutlery available to use your right hand to eat, as using your left hand will cause great offence.

SOUTH-EAST ASIA

Around breakfast time in countries like Vietnam, Cambodia and Thailand you will find the locals enjoying rice noodle soups called pho, foe or kyteow, depending on where you are. These soups are a brilliant way to start your day and are also useful, inexpensive snacks in-between meals.

For other meals, people generally eat the more traditional meats such as chicken and pork, with vegetables and sticky rice or fresh, spicy salads.

In this region, fresh herbs such as lemongrass, basil, coriander, mint and chilli are plentiful, as are fish sauce, soy sauce and lime juice.

In Thailand you'll come across some wonderful curries made from thick, spicy pastes combined with coconut cream or milk.

There are some incredible bakeries in countries like Vietnam, who learned the trade from the French during their occupation.

If you're feeling daring, try the fermented fish paste prahoc in Cambodia, or perhaps a three-quarter term egg in Vietnam, which certainly has a crunch!

Australia and New Zealand

As relatively young countries, Australia and New Zealand may not have many traditional recipes, but that does not stop them producing some outstanding food. Their climates allow them both to produce a wide range of ingredients, most notably their internationally renowned livestock, including sheep and cattle. Also, the vast coastlines provide some of the best seafood in the world.

Their historical links to Europe combined with their close proximity to South East Asia has developed a 'fusion' cooking style which gives fresh local produce a twist.

Barbeques are a part of everyday life in this part of the world, mainly because of the temperate climate and outdoor lifestyle. You'll be able to purchase kangaroo at most supermarkets and may also find emu or crocodile on some menus in Australia.

Both countries are renowned for their 'new world' wines. They also produce some fantastic beers including Coopers, Cascade and Steinlager.

Hokey pokey ice cream (the New Zealand version of honeycomb) and lamingtons (Australian sponge cakes covered in chocolate and coconut) are worth a try if you have a sweet tooth! Both countries lay claim to the world famous pavlova, but either way it is a dessert worth trying. You'll also be able to enjoy a wide range of tropical fruits such as mangoes, pineapples, melons and kiwi fruit.

The Americas

UNITED STATES OF AMERICA AND CANADA

Many might think of the States as a fast food nation but, travelling around the country, you will be able to sample every type of cuisine imaginable.

In the South, you will come across food like grits (corn porridge), corn bread, fried chicken and black-eyed peas as well as a range of Creole dishes such as gumbo and jambalaya. Closer to the Mexican border you'll come across Tex-Mex style cooking which includes enchiladas, burritos and chilli con carne.

In the Midwest, you'll see why Americans are the largest consumers of beef in the world. This is the place for carnivores; you'll be able to get stuck into barbequed meats, sausages, ribs and pot roasts.

One thing you must do is visit a local diner for an all American breakfast. You will be treated to an endless choice of pancakes, bacon, sausages, waffles, eggs and hash browns, all topped with maple syrup.

Don't forget, this is the nation that invented the super-size, so expect portions to be a fair bit larger than you're used to.

CENTRAL AMERICA AND MEXICO

Much Central American food is based on its Mayan and Aztec heritage and incorporates native ingredients such as chillies, corn, tomatoes, peppers, beans, plantains and tomatillos.

Beans are also extremely popular, and make up many of the staple dishes such as frijoles (slow-cooked beans) and pupusas (griddle cakes stuffed with beans and cheese). Pork is the most common meat so you will find plenty of dishes made using pork loin, bacon and ribs.

Many dishes are accompanied by tortilla breads or chips, and a range of salsas and other condiments including the famous guacamole.

Mexicans were the first to discover chocolate and traditionally concocted drinks combining the bitter chocolate with honey, nuts, seeds and spices. You will also find it is a key ingredient in the sauce mole, which contains chillies, garlic, nuts, tomato, spices and chocolate.

While in Mexico, try a traditional margarita or just slowly sip tequila as you'd enjoy a fine wine.

SOUTH AMERICA

In Brazil, a number of 'pay by the kilo' buffet restaurants display everything from seafood and grills, to chips and desserts. Be sure to try a churrasco, where skewers of meat are carried from table to table and sliced directly onto your plate.

Argentina is a steak lover's heaven and you'll be lucky if you manage a single night without beef during your stay in the country. If you like chocolate, be sure to visit Bariloche, which was founded by Swiss immigrants. This gorgeous lakeside town has a number of chocolate shops and is also known for its fondue.

The local specialty of Peru is alpaca, a relative of the llama, and guinea pig, which is carried to your table complete with a celery hat and a cherry tomato in its mouth. This is certainly not for the feint of heart! If you're not feeling adventurous, there are plenty of restaurants offering basic pizzas and the obligatory jamon y queso toasted sandwich.

The further north you go, the more the ingredients reflect neighbouring Central America, such as corn and avocado. In Colombia, you will find a traditional dish called ajiaco, which is a soup made of chicken, corn, avocado and potatoes served with white rice and fresh herb salad.

Both Argentina and Chile produce excellent wines, most notably the local favourite Malbec, and there are some great cocktails including caiprinha in Brazil and pisco sour in Peru. If you're looking for something non-alcoholic, try Inca Kola in Peru or the world-famous coffee in Colombia.

Snacks and Soups

French Onion Soup see page 37

Bruschetta

Serves 2

WHAT YOU'LL NEED:

Ingredients
2 slices crusty bread
 (1.5 cm/⅔ in thick)
1 garlic clove
2 large tomatoes, chopped
1 small red onion, chopped
1 teaspoon olive oil
Salt and pepper
Handful fresh basil

Equipment
Oven grill
Chopping board
Sharp knife
Small bowl
Teaspoon

WHAT TO DO:

Place the bread under a hot oven grill and toast on both sides until golden brown. Cut the garlic clove in half and rub it straight onto the toasted bread.

Mix together the tomatoes and onion in a small bowl with the olive oil, salt and pepper. Tear up the basil and add to the mix.

Spoon the mixture onto the toasted bread.

Chorizo and Beans

Serves 2

WHAT YOU'LL NEED:

Ingredients	Equipment
1 tablespoon olive oil	Stove top
100 g/4 oz chorizo, cut into 1 cm/½ in slices	Large frying pan
1 small onion, finely chopped	Chopping board
1 clove garlic, crushed	Sharp knife
1 chilli, deseeded and finely chopped	Can opener
400 g/14 oz can white beans, drained	Tablespoon
Juice of half a lemon	
1 tablespoon parsley, chopped	
Salt and pepper	

WHAT TO DO:

Heat the oil in a frying pan over a medium–high heat. Add the chorizo and cook for about 5 minutes, stirring, until it is lightly browned and crispy on the outside.

Remove the chorizo from the frying pan leaving the flavoured oil behind. Add the onion and cook gently for about 5 minutes, then add the garlic and chilli and cook for a further 2 minutes.

Return the chorizo to the frying pan, add the beans and heat through, stirring to incorporate all the flavours.

Remove the frying pan from the heat and stir in the lemon juice, parsley and seasoning and serve immediately.

Flatbread Pizza with Rosemary and Garlic

Serves 2

WHAT YOU'LL NEED:

Ingredients	Equipment
2 flatbreads/pita breads	Oven
1 clove garlic, finely chopped	Baking tray
2 tablespoons rosemary, finely chopped	Chopping board
Salt	Sharp knife
2 tablespoons olive oil (preferably virgin)	Tablespoon

WHAT TO DO:

Preheat the oven to 200°C/400°F/gas mark 6.

Place the flatbreads/pita breads on a baking tray and sprinkle over the garlic, rosemary and salt to taste. Drizzle with the olive oil.

Bake the pizzas for 3–5 minutes or until golden brown and crispy.

Cut each pizza into 8 pieces and serve immediately.

Guacamole

Serves 2

WHAT YOU'LL NEED:

Ingredients
1 avocado
1 small tomato, finely chopped
1 small red onion, finely chopped
½ large chilli, deseeded and
   finely chopped
1 tablespoon lemon juice
1 tablespoon oil

Equipment
Small bowl
Tablespoon
Fork

WHAT TO DO:

Cut the avocado in half, scoop out the flesh and mash with a fork.

Add the other ingredients and mix well.

Serve the dip with corn chips or carrot and celery sticks.

Mexican Scrambled Eggs

Serves 2

WHAT YOU'LL NEED:

Ingredients
2 tablespoons olive oil
4 small or 2 large tortillas,
   cut into thin strips
2 tablespoons butter
2 large tomatoes, chopped
1 small onion, finely chopped
1 small green chilli, deseeded
   and finely chopped
6 eggs, beaten
Salt and pepper

Equipment
Stove top
Frying pan
Chopping board
Sharp knife
Tablespoon
Small bowl

WHAT TO DO:

Heat the oil in a frying pan and add the tortilla strips. Cook for a few minutes until the tortillas are crispy and browned. Remove from the frying pan and set aside.

Heat the butter in the frying pan and add the tomato, onion and chilli. Cook for 2 minutes.

Place the eggs in a bowl and beat. Pour the eggs over the other ingredients and stir until the mixture starts to thicken.

Remove from the heat and fold through the crispy tortilla strips. Season with salt and pepper to taste.

Nachos

Serves 2

WHAT YOU'LL NEED:

Ingredients
200 g/7 oz pack corn chips
200 g/7 oz jar tomato salsa
2 cups grated cheese
1 tablespoon jalapeno peppers,
  chopped (optional)
60 ml/2 fl oz/¼ cup sour cream
  or guacamole

Equipment
Oven
Ovenproof dish
Chopping board
Sharp knife
Tablespoon

WHAT TO DO:
Preheat the oven to 180°C/350°F/gas mark 4.

Place half the corn chips in an ovenproof dish, pour over half the
salsa and sprinkle with half the cheese. If using jalapeno peppers,
scatter them over the cheese. Repeat the layers of corn chips,
salsa and cheese.

Bake the nachos for about 10–15 minutes or until the cheese
has melted.

Serve the nachos topped with the sour cream or a blob of
guacamole dip.

Omelette

Serves 1

WHAT YOU'LL NEED (PER SERVING):

Ingredients	Equipment
2 eggs	Stove top
1 tablespoon water	Frying pan (preferably non-stick)
Salt and pepper	Small bowl
1 tablespoon butter	Tablespoon
Any filling you wish (e.g. grated cheese, fresh herbs, chopped ham, sliced tomatoes, sliced mushrooms)	Spatula

WHAT TO DO:

Place the eggs, water and seasoning in a bowl and whisk until slightly frothy.

Melt the butter in a frying pan over a medium–high heat, swirling it around to coat the surface. When the frying pan is hot and the butter sizzles pour in the egg mixture.

Using the spatula, quickly stir the egg mixture so the cooked egg is drawn towards the centre, then tilt the pan outwards so the uncooked egg runs to the edge. Repeat this process until the omelette is nearly set.

Sprinkle your chosen filling over one half of the omelette and gently lift the other half over to create a half-moon shape. Slide the omelette onto a plate and serve immediately.

Pizza Subs

WHAT YOU'LL NEED:

Ingredients	Equipment
1 large breadstick	Oven grill
2 tablespoons tomato purée	Chopping board
Any pizza topping you wish (e.g. sliced salami, ham, pineapple chunks, peppers, mushrooms)	Sharp knife
	Tablespoon
	Cup
Handful cheese, grated	

WHAT TO DO:

Slice the breadstick in half and spread the tomato purée on the insides of the bread.

Layer your preferred pizza toppings evenly across the tomato purée and then sprinkle over the cheese.

Place the pizza subs under an oven grill at a high temperature. When the cheese has melted, take the pizza subs out and let them cool slightly before eating.

Potato Wedges

Serves 2

WHAT YOU'LL NEED:

Ingredients	Equipment
2–3 medium potatoes	Oven
1–2 tablespoons olive oil	Baking tray
Salt and pepper	Chopping board
	Sharp knife
	Tablespoon

WHAT TO DO:

Preheat the oven to 220°C/425°F/gas mark 7.

Cut each potato into quarters lengthways and then cut each piece in half so you end up with 8 wedges. Don't bother peeling them as the skin adds lots of flavour. Place the potatoes on a baking tray and drizzle with oil.

Bake the potatoes for 20 minutes, turn over and cook for a further 20 minutes or until golden brown on the outside and soft in the middle. Remove the wedges from the oven and sprinkle with salt and pepper. Note: Great served with tomato salsa and sour cream.

Bean and Tomato Soup

Serves 2

WHAT YOU'LL NEED:

Ingredients	Equipment
1 tablespoon olive oil	Stove top
1 onion, finely chopped	Saucepan
1 clove garlic, finely chopped	Can opener
400 g/14 oz can chopped tomatoes	Chopping board
400 g/14 oz can white beans,	Sharp knife
drained and rinsed	Tablespoon
500 ml/16 fl oz/2 cups chicken stock	Teaspoon
1 teaspoon dried Italian herbs	
Salt and pepper	
Handful parmesan cheese, grated	

WHAT TO DO:

Heat the oil in a saucepan, add the onion and garlic and cook for 5 minutes.

Add the tomatoes, beans, stock and seasoning and bring to the boil.

Reduce the heat and simmer for about 15 minutes. Add a little water if the soup is too thick.

Ladle the soup into 2 bowls and sprinkle with cheese.

Chicken Noodle Soup

Serves 2

WHAT YOU'LL NEED:

Ingredients
750 ml/25 fl oz/3 cups water
1 chicken breast, cut into
    1.5 cm/⅔ in strips
2 packets chicken 2 minute
    noodles (85 g/3 oz each)
1 spring onion, finely sliced
6 snow peas, finely sliced

Equipment
Stove top
Saucepan
Chopping board
Sharp knife

WHAT TO DO:
Pour the water into a saucepan and add the seasoning sachets from
the packets of 2 minute noodles. Bring the liquid to the boil. Add the
chicken pieces and simmer gently for 8–10 minutes or until the
chicken is cooked.

Add the noodles, spring onion and snow peas, stirring well to break up
the noodles. Simmer for 2 minutes and serve immediately.

Corn Chowder

Serves 2

WHAT YOU'LL NEED:

Ingredients
1 tablespoon butter
1 onion, finely chopped
½ green pepper, finely chopped
1 potato, finely chopped
400 g/14 oz can creamed corn
750 ml/25 fl oz/3 cups milk
Salt and pepper

Equipment
Stove top
Saucepan
Can opener
Chopping board
Sharp knife
Tablespoon

WHAT TO DO:

Melt the butter in a saucepan and add the onion, pepper and potato.
Cook gently over a low heat for 15 minutes or until the vegetables
are tender but not browned.

Add the corn, milk and seasoning and slowly bring to the boil, stirring
to mix all the ingredients together. Simmer for 5 minutes and serve.

Crushed Pea and Mint Soup

Serves 2

WHAT YOU'LL NEED:

Ingredients

3 cups frozen green peas

1 large potato, peeled and
  finely chopped

2 spring onions, finely chopped

750 ml/25 fl oz/3 cups
  chicken stock

60 ml/2 fl oz/¼ cup cream

1 tablespoon fresh mint,
  finely chopped

Salt and pepper

Equipment

Stove top

Saucepan with lid

Bowl

Chopping board

Sharp knife

Tablespoon

Cup

WHAT TO DO:

Place the peas, potato, spring onions and stock in a saucepan and bring to the boil. Cover and simmer for 10 minutes or until the potatoes are tender.

Drain the liquid into a bowl and crush the peas and potatoes with a fork or potato masher.

Return the liquid to the saucepan along with the cream, mint and seasoning and heat through, stirring regularly.

French Onion Soup

Serves 2

WHAT YOU'LL NEED:

Ingredients	Equipment
2 tablespoons butter	Stove top
2 large onions, thinly sliced	Oven grill
1 clove garlic, crushed	Saucepan with lid
750 ml/25 fl oz/3 cups beef stock	Grater
Pepper	Tablespoon
2 slices French stick	
(1.5 cm/⅔ in thick)	
Handful cheese, grated	

WHAT TO DO:

Melt the butter in a saucepan over a medium heat. Add the onions and cook for about 20 minutes, stirring occasionally, until tender and caramelized. Add the garlic and cook for a further 2 minutes.

Pour the stock into the saucepan, add a pinch of pepper and bring to the boil. Reduce the heat, cover and simmer for about 15 minutes.

Meanwhile toast the bread on one side under the oven grill. Turn over and sprinkle the other side evenly with cheese, then place back under grill until the cheese melts.

Pour the soup into 2 bowls and float a piece of the toasted bread, cheese side up, in each bowl.

Mushroom Soup

Serves 2

WHAT YOU'LL NEED:

Ingredients
2 tablespoons butter
1 small onion, thinly sliced
1 clove garlic, crushed
3 cups mushrooms, sliced
750 ml/25 fl oz/3 cups
   chicken stock
Pepper
2 tablespoons parsley,
   chopped (optional)

Equipment
Stove top
Saucepan with lid
Chopping board
Sharp knife
Tablespoon
Cup

WHAT TO DO:

Melt the butter in a saucepan over a medium heat. Add the onion and cook for about 5 minutes, stirring occasionally. Add the garlic and mushrooms and cook for a further 5 minutes.

Pour the stock into the saucepan and add a pinch of pepper. Bring to the boil, reduce the heat, cover and simmer for about 15 minutes. Ladle the soup into 2 bowls and sprinkle the parsley over the top.

Chicken Dishes

Parmesan Drumsticks see page 54

How to Cook Chicken

Chicken is one of the easiest cuts of meat to cook; as long as you cook the meat for long enough you really can't go wrong. You will come across the following cuts of chicken:

BREASTS

This is the most common cut of chicken. It is boneless and will come with either the skin on or skin off. To cook chicken breast, you can fry it in oil on a stove for about 6 minutes on each side, or bake it in an oven for about 20 minutes on a medium heat (180°C/350°F/gas mark 4).

THIGHS

This darker meat is the tastiest part of the chicken and it is cheaper to buy than breasts. You can either cut the chicken meat away from the bones and cook it in a similar style to chicken breast, or you can cook the chicken on the bone, but this will take a little bit longer to cook through.

DRUMSTICKS

These are similar to thighs but easier to eat, particularly when cold. However, they usually take around 45 minutes to cook in a medium oven so you'll need to allow time for this.

WINGS

These make a great snack or starter and can be enjoyed by coating them in a pre-bought marinade or just by using a combination of oil, chilli and garlic. Simply pan fry them for 5 minutes at a high heat or bake in the oven for about 20–30 minutes.

When cooking chicken, you must always make sure the meat is cooked right through. To check, make a small cut into the thickest part of the meat and, if it is still pink, keep cooking for another couple of minutes. When it is ready it will have turned white and the juices will run clear.

Baked Chicken and Mushrooms

Serves 2

WHAT YOU'LL NEED:

Ingredients	Equipment
2 chicken breasts	Oven
2 tablespoons olive oil	Shallow ovenproof dish
Salt and pepper	Chopping board
1 teaspoon dried Italian herbs	Sharp knife
1 clove garlic, finely chopped	Tablespoon
1 cup mushrooms, sliced	Teaspoon
Handful parmesan cheese, grated	Grater
	Cup
	Aluminium foil

WHAT TO DO:

Preheat the oven to 180°C/350°F/gas mark 4.

Pound the chicken breasts with a heavy object (e.g. meat mallet, rolling pin, base of a saucepan) to reduce the thickness. Pour half the oil into an ovenproof dish, add the chicken and sprinkle with the salt, pepper, herbs and garlic.

Spread the mushrooms evenly over the chicken and sprinkle with cheese. Drizzle the remaining oil over the top and cover the dish with foil.

Bake the chicken for 15 minutes. Remove the foil and bake for a further 10 minutes or until the chicken is cooked through and browned on top.

Baked Chicken with Green Olives   Serves 2

WHAT YOU'LL NEED:

Ingredients	Equipment
¼ cup green olives, pitted and finely chopped	Oven
1 tablespoon parsley, finely chopped	Shallow ovenproof dish
1 clove garlic, finely chopped	Small bowl
1 tablespoon olive oil	Chopping board
1 tablespoon lemon juice	Sharp knife
2 chicken breasts	Tablespoon

WHAT TO DO:

Preheat the oven to 180°C/350°C/gas mark 4.

Combine the olives, parsley, garlic, oil and lemon juice in a bowl and mix thoroughly.

Place the chicken in an ovenproof dish and spread the olive mixture over it.

Bake the chicken for about 25 minutes or until cooked through.

Chicken and Bacon Burgers

Serves 2

WHAT YOU'LL NEED:

Ingredients
2 tablespoons olive oil
2 bacon rashers, chopped
2 chicken breasts
1 clove garlic, crushed
2 burger buns, halved
Half an avocado, sliced
Mayonnaise
Any toppings you wish (e.g. sliced
    tomatoes, shredded lettuce,
    cheese slices, etc.)

Equipment
Stove top
Frying pan
Grater
Chopping board
Sharp knife
Tablespoon
Cling film

WHAT TO DO:

Heat half the oil in a frying pan and cook the bacon on a high heat until crisp. Remove and set aside.

Place the chicken between 2 sheets of cling film and pound with a heavy object (e.g. meat mallet, rolling pin, base of a saucepan) to flatten. Rub the garlic and remaining oil over the chicken.

Heat the frying pan on a medium–high heat (don't add any oil) and cook the chicken for 3–4 minutes, then turn over and cook the other side for 3–4 minutes or until chicken is cooked through.

Remove the chicken from the frying pan and place in the buns, top with the bacon, avocado and mayonnaise and any other toppings of your choice.

Chicken Cacciatore

Serves 2

WHAT YOU'LL NEED:

Ingredients
2 tablespoons oil
4 chicken thighs, cut into
   1.5 cm/$\frac{2}{3}$ in pieces
1 medium onion, chopped
1 small green pepper, chopped
2 cloves garlic, crushed
400 g/14 oz can chopped tomatoes
1 teaspoon dried Italian herbs
10 black olives, pitted and halved

Equipment
Stove top
Large frying pan with lid
Can opener
Chopping board
Sharp knife
Tablespoon
Teaspoon

WHAT TO DO:

Heat half the oil in a frying pan and cook the chicken until browned on the outside. Remove and set aside.

Pour the remaining oil in the frying pan and cook the onion, pepper and garlic over a medium heat for 10 minutes or until browned and softened. Add the tomatoes, herbs and olives and cook for 10 minutes.

Place the chicken pieces back in the frying pan and stir through the sauce. If the sauce is too thick add a little water. Cover the frying pan and cook on a low heat for about 10 minutes or until the chicken is cooked through.

Chicken Curry

Serves 2

WHAT YOU'LL NEED:

Ingredients	Equipment
2 tablespoons oil	Stove top
1 small onion, chopped	Saucepan with lid
1 small red pepper, chopped	Chopping board
1 clove garlic, finely chopped	Sharp knife
2 cm/¾ in piece fresh ginger,	Tablespoon
finely chopped	Cup
1 tablespoon curry powder	
185 ml/6 fl oz/¾ cup chicken stock	
1 tomato, chopped	
4 chicken thighs, cut into	
1.5 cm/⅔ in pieces	
1 handful spinach, chopped	
2 tablespoons natural yoghurt	

WHAT TO DO:

Heat the oil in a saucepan and cook the onion, pepper and garlic over a medium heat for 10 minutes or until browned and softened. Add the ginger and curry powder and cook, stirring, for 2 minutes.

Add the stock and tomato and bring to the boil. Reduce the heat, add the chicken, cover the saucepan and simmer for 5 minutes. Remove the lid, add the spinach and cook for a further 5 minutes or until chicken is cooked through.

Take the saucepan off the heat, stir in the yoghurt and serve with rice.

Chicken Fajitas

Serves 2

WHAT YOU'LL NEED:

Ingredients
1 tablespoon jalapeno peppers,
  chopped
1 garlic clove, crushed
4 tablespoons fresh lime juice
2 chicken breasts, cut into
  1.5 cm/⅔ in strips
1 tablespoon olive oil
1 pepper (any colour), thinly sliced
1 onion, thinly sliced
4 tortillas
Your choice of sour cream,
  salsa or guacamole dip

Equipment
Stove top
Oven grill or microwave
Saucepan
Bowl
Chopping board
Sharp knife

WHAT TO DO:

Mix the jalapeno peppers, garlic and lime juice in a bowl. Add the chicken and stir until coated. If possible, cover and leave to marinate for 30 minutes.

Heat the oil in a saucepan and add the peppers and onion. Cook for 5 minutes until they start to soften. Add the chicken and cook for another 10 minutes until the chicken is browned and cooked through.

Place the tortillas under the grill or in the microwave for 2 minutes, until they are hot. Spoon the chicken and pepper mixture onto each tortilla.

Add either sour cream, salsa or guacamole dip. Roll up the tortilla and serve.

Chicken Parmigiana

Serves 2

WHAT YOU'LL NEED:

Ingredients
125 ml/4 fl oz/½ cup tomato
   purée/passata
1 clove garlic, crushed
½ teaspoon dried Italian herbs
Salt and pepper
2 chicken breasts
Handful mozzarella cheese, grated

Equipment
Oven
Shallow ovenproof dish
Small bowl
Grater
Teaspoon
Cup

WHAT TO DO:
Preheat the oven to 180°C/350°F/gas mark 4.

Combine the tomato purée, garlic, herbs and seasoning in a bowl.

Pound the chicken breasts with a heavy object (e.g. meat mallet, rolling pin, base of a saucepan) to reduce the thickness.

Place the chicken in an ovenproof dish and spoon the tomato mixture over the top. Sprinkle with the cheese.

Bake the chicken for about 25 minutes or until cooked through.

Chicken Quesadillas

Serves 2

WHAT YOU'LL NEED:

Ingredients

1 tablespoon oil
2 chicken breasts, cut into
    1.5 cm/$^2/_3$ in strips
4 tortillas
Handful cheese, grated
1 tomato, chopped
2 tablespoons black olives, pitted
    and chopped
1 tablespoon sour cream

Equipment

Stove top
Frying pan
Chopping board
Sharp knife
Tablespoon
Spatula

WHAT TO DO:

Heat the oil in a frying pan and cook the chicken until golden brown.
Remove and set aside.

Turn the frying pan down to a medium heat and place a tortilla in it.
Sprinkle half the cheese evenly across the tortilla and then add half
the diced tomatoes and olives.

Layer half the chicken over the top of the cheese, tomatoes and
olives and then top with another tortilla.

Using a spatula, flip the entire tortilla over and cook on the other
side until the cheese is melted. Repeat the process to make the
second tortilla.

Serve with sour cream.

Chicken and Vegetable Stack

Serves 2

WHAT YOU'LL NEED:

Ingredients
2 slices aubergine/eggplant
   (1.5 cm/²⁄₃ in thick)
2 tomatoes (roma if possible),
   thickly sliced
2 chicken breasts
Handful parmesan cheese, grated
Handful mozzarella cheese, grated

Equipment
Oven
Baking tray or dish
Chopping board
Sharp knife

WHAT TO DO:
Preheat the oven to 180°C/350°F/gas mark 4.

Place the slices of aubergine/eggplant onto a greased baking tray and then add a layer of tomatoes on top. Place the chicken on top of the tomatoes and sprinkle with a mixture of the two cheeses.

Bake the chicken for about 25 minutes or until cooked through.

Chicken Wings with Lime and Chilli   Serves 2

WHAT YOU'LL NEED:

Ingredients
Juice of 1 lime
1 tablespoon oil
1 clove garlic, crushed
2 cm/¾ in piece fresh ginger,
  finely chopped
1 chilli, deseeded and
  finely chopped
8 chicken wings

Equipment
Oven
Baking tray or ovenproof dish
Large bowl (not plastic)
Chopping board
Sharp knife
Teaspoon

WHAT TO DO:
Preheat the oven to 200°C/400°F/gas mark 6.

Combine the lime juice, oil, garlic, ginger and chilli in a bowl.
Add the chicken and turn to coat evenly. Cover and refrigerate
for as long as possible.

Place the chicken wings on a baking tray and cook for approximately
20–30 minutes or until golden brown and cooked through.

Chicken Wrapped in Prosciutto

Serves 2

WHAT YOU'LL NEED:

Ingredients	Equipment
2 chicken breasts	Stove top
Handful cheese, grated	Frying pan
4 slices prosciutto	Grater
1 tablespoon olive oil	Chopping board
	Sharp knife
	Cling film

WHAT TO DO:

Place the chicken breasts on a chopping board and sprinkle with cheese. Top each piece of chicken with prosciutto.

Place the chicken between 2 sheets of cling film and pound with a heavy object (e.g. meat mallet, rolling pin, base of a saucepan) to flatten.

Heat the oil in a frying pan and place the chicken in prosciutto-side down first.

Cook for 4–5 minutes and then turn over and cook the other side for 4–5 minutes or until chicken is cooked through.

Chilli Chicken Stir-fry

Serves 2

WHAT YOU'LL NEED:

Ingredients

2 tablespoons oil
2 chicken breasts, cut into
   1.5 cm/⅔ in strips
1 small onion, thinly sliced
1 small red pepper, thinly sliced
1 small carrot, thinly sliced
1 chilli, deseeded and finely chopped
1 clove garlic, finely chopped
2 cm/¾ in piece fresh ginger,
  finely chopped
2 tablespoons soy sauce
2 tablespoons boiling water
2 tablespoons fresh basil

Equipment

Stove top
Large frying pan
Chopping board
Sharp knife
Tablespoon

WHAT TO DO:

Heat half the oil in a frying pan over a high heat until it is smoking
hot. Add the chicken strips and stir-fry for a couple of minutes until
browned and cooked through. Remove the chicken from the frying
pan and set aside.

Pour the remaining oil into the frying pan and reduce the heat so that it
is medium–high. Add the vegetables, chilli, garlic and ginger and stir-fry
for a few minutes until browned and softened. If required, add some
water to prevent the vegetables from burning before they are cooked.

Return the chicken to the frying pan, add the soy sauce and boiling
water and stir until warmed through. Tear the basil into pieces, add to
the chicken and vegetables and serve immediately with rice.

Creamy Chicken and Spinach

Serves 2

WHAT YOU'LL NEED:

Ingredients	Equipment
2 tablespoons olive oil	Stove top
2 bacon rashers, chopped	Frying pan with lid
2 chicken breasts, cut into 1.5 cm/²/₃ in pieces	Small bowl
1 handful spinach, chopped	Chopping board
110 g/4 oz cream cheese	Sharp knife
1 garlic clove, crushed	Tablespoon
1 teaspoon dried Italian herbs	Teaspoon
Salt and pepper	
4 tablespoons water	

WHAT TO DO:

Heat half the oil in a frying pan and cook the bacon on a high heat until crisp. Remove and set aside.

Heat the remaining oil in the frying pan and cook the chicken until browned on the outside. Add the spinach.

Meanwhile, combine the cream cheese, garlic, herbs, seasoning and water in a small bowl and stir until smooth.

Pour the cheese mixture over the chicken and spinach and stir to combine. Cover with a lid and slowly bring the sauce to the boil. Reduce the heat and simmer gently for about 10 minutes until the chicken is cooked through. Add a little more water if required. Serve the chicken with the bacon pieces scattered over the top.

Parmesan Drumsticks

Serves 2

WHAT YOU'LL NEED:

Ingredients	Equipment
2 handfuls parmesan cheese, grated	Oven
	Baking tray or ovenproof dish
Salt and pepper	2 shallow dishes
1 egg white	Grater
6 chicken drumsticks	Cup

WHAT TO DO:

Preheat the oven to 200°C/400°F/gas mark 6.

Mix together the cheese, salt and pepper in a shallow dish. In a separate dish, beat the egg white until fluffy. Dip the chicken in the egg white and coat well, then roll in the cheese mixture.

Place the chicken on a baking tray and bake for approximately 45 minutes or until golden brown and cooked through.

Sticky Chicken Wings

Serves 2

WHAT YOU'LL NEED:

Ingredients	Equipment
8 chicken wings	Stove top
2 cm/¾ in piece fresh ginger, finely chopped	Saucepan
1 can cola	Frying pan
1 tablespoon oil	Chopping board
	Sharp knife

WHAT TO DO:

Place the chicken wings and ginger in a saucepan and pour in enough cola to cover the chicken. Boil for about 10 minutes until almost all the liquid has evaporated.

Heat the oil in a frying pan and transfer the chicken wings along with any remaining cola. Cook over a high heat for 3–5 minutes, turning frequently, until the wings have browned and the sauce has become thick and sticky.

Meat Dishes

Greek Lamb Chops see page 69

How to Cook Meat

Red meat, including beef and lamb, can be cooked to personal preference, for example rare, medium or well done. Pork is usually cooked in a similar way to chicken, so that it's cooked through but not too dry. Processed meats like sausages should always be cooked right through.

BEEF STEAKS

To cook the perfect steak, you need to make sure the frying pan is really hot and remember not to put any oil in the pan. Instead, drizzle a small amount of oil directly onto the steak and season with salt and pepper. Add the steak to the frying pan and cook until it's to your liking – roughly 2 minutes on each side for rare, 3 minutes for medium and 5 minutes for well done.

CHOPS

The easiest way to cook lamb chops is to pan fry them on a high heat for about 4 minutes on each side. Alternatively, you can pan fry them for 1–2 minutes, so that the meat goes golden brown, and then put them in the oven to cook through for 10 minutes. Try brushing them with garlic and fresh rosemary before cooking.

FILLETS

Pork and lamb fillets can be cooked the same way as chops, by browning them on the stove and then placing them in the oven to cook through.

MINCE

Cooking mince will usually be the first step in a recipe you are following such as spaghetti bolognaise or cottage pie. Mince doesn't require any preparation, you just need to place it in a pan on the stove with some olive oil and watch as the pink meat turns brown. Make sure you stir it from time to time to break up any lumps and ensure the meat is cooked through.

Always try to 'rest' red meat after you've cooked it, this means leaving it to sit for a few minutes before eating. This allows all of the juices that have come out of the meat during the cooking process to soak back in again, which increases tenderness and flavour!

Chorizo and Chickpea Stew

Serves 2

WHAT YOU'LL NEED:

Ingredients	Equipment
1 tablespoon olive oil	Stove top
1 small onion, thinly sliced	Frying pan
100 g/4 oz chorizo, cut into	Can opener
1 cm/½ in slices	Chopping board
1 clove garlic, crushed	Sharp knife
400 g/14 oz can chopped tomatoes	Tablespoon
400 g/14 oz can chickpeas, drained	

WHAT TO DO:

Heat the oil in a frying pan, add the onion and cook for 5 minutes or until softened. Add the chorizo and garlic and cook over a low heat for 5 minutes.

Stir in the tomatoes and chickpeas. Half fill the can with water and add to the pan. Bring to the boil and cook on a high heat for 10 minutes until the stew thickens.

Serve with crusty bread.

Beef Stroganoff

Serves 2

WHAT YOU'LL NEED:

Ingredients

2 tablespoons olive oil
250 g/9 oz beef steak, cut into
   1.5 cm/²⁄₃ in strips
1 small brown onion, thinly sliced
1 clove garlic, finely chopped
1 cup mushrooms, thinly sliced
1 tablespoon tomato paste
1 teaspoon paprika
⅓ cup water
60 ml/2 fl oz/¼ cup sour cream

Equipment

Stove top
Frying pan
Chopping board
Sharp knife
Tablespoon
Cup

WHAT TO DO:

Heat half the oil in a frying pan over a high heat. Add the beef and cook, stirring, for about 3 minutes or until browned. Remove the meat and set aside.

Heat the remaining oil in the frying pan, add the onion and garlic and cook over a gentle heat for about 5 minutes until just coloured.

Add the mushrooms, tomato paste and paprika and cook for a further 3 minutes or until the mushrooms are tender.

Return the meat to the frying pan along with the water and bring the sauce to the boil. Lower the heat, add the sour cream and stir for a couple of minutes to heat through.

Serve with boiled rice or noodles.

Chilli Con Carne

Serves 2

WHAT YOU'LL NEED:

Ingredients	Equipment
1 teaspoon olive oil	Stove top
1 onion, chopped	Saucepan with lid
250 g/9 oz minced beef	Can opener
400 g/14 oz can chopped tomatoes	Chopping board
400 g/14 oz can red kidney beans, drained and rinsed	Sharp knife
1 teaspoon chilli powder	Teaspoon

WHAT TO DO:

Heat the oil in a saucepan, add the onion and cook for 5 minutes or until softened.

Add the minced meat and cook until the meat has turned brown, stirring constantly to break up any lumps. Add the tomatoes, beans and chilli powder.

Put the lid on the saucepan and bring to the boil. Lower the heat and simmer for 20 minutes.

Serve with rice.

Chow Mein

Serves 2

WHAT YOU'LL NEED:

Ingredients

1 tablespoon oil
250 g/9 oz minced beef or pork
12 green beans, sliced into
  2.5 cm/1 in pieces
150 g/5 oz cabbage, thinly sliced
1 small onion, thinly chopped
1 clove garlic, finely chopped
1.5 cm/²⁄₃ in piece fresh ginger,
  finely chopped
½ teaspoon curry powder
2 minute chicken noodles
1 cup boiling water

Equipment

Stove top
Large saucepan
Chopping board
Sharp knife
Tablespoon
Teaspoon
Cup

WHAT TO DO:

Heat the oil in a saucepan, add the minced meat and cook until the meat has turned brown, stirring constantly to break up any lumps.

Add the beans, cabbage, onion, garlic, ginger, curry powder and sachet from the 2 minute chicken noodles. Stir for 2–3 minutes and then add the noodles (broken into smaller pieces) and boiling water. Simmer for about 8 minutes, stirring regularly, and then serve.

Cottage Pie

Serves 2

WHAT YOU'LL NEED:

Ingredients	Equipment
Savoury mince (see page 68)	Stove top
2 large potatoes, peeled	Oven
and quartered	Saucepan
1 tablespoon butter	Ovenproof dish
60 ml/2 fl oz/¼ cup milk	Chopping board
Salt and pepper	Sharp knife
	Tablespoon
	Cup

WHAT TO DO:

Preheat the oven to 180°C/350°F/gas mark 4.

Prepare the savoury mince as per the recipe.

In the meantime, cook the potatoes in boiling water until tender
and then drain. Add the butter, milk and seasoning and mash
until smooth.

Pour the meat mixture into a greased baking dish and spoon the
mashed potato on top. Use a fork to rough up the top of the potato.

Bake for 20 minutes.

Garlic Beef Stir-fry

Serves 2

WHAT YOU'LL NEED:

Ingredients
2 tablespoons vegetable oil
250 g/9 oz steak, cut into
    1.5 cm/⅔ in strips
1 small onion, sliced
1 small red pepper, sliced
2 cloves garlic, finely chopped
2 tablespoons soy sauce
2 tablespoons boiling water

Equipment
Stove top
Large frying pan
Chopping board
Sharp knife
Tablespoon

WHAT TO DO:

Heat half the oil in a frying pan over a high heat until it is smoking hot. Add the steak strips and stir-fry for a couple of minutes until browned. Remove the meat from the frying pan and set aside.

Pour the remaining oil into the frying pan and reduce the heat to medium–high. Add the onion and pepper and stir-fry for a few minutes until browned and soft. Add the garlic and stir-fry for 1 minute.

Return the meat to the frying pan, add the soy sauce and boiling water and stir until warmed through. Serve immediately with rice.

Hamburgers

Serves 2

WHAT YOU'LL NEED:

Ingredients	Equipment
1 small onion	Stove top
250 g/9 oz lean minced beef	Frying pan
1 clove garlic, finely chopped	Bowl
Salt and pepper	Chopping board
½ teaspoon dried Italian herbs	Sharp knife
1 tablespoon olive oil	Tablespoon
2 hamburger buns, cut in half	Teaspoon
Sauce of your choice	
Any toppings you wish (e.g. sliced tomatoes, shredded lettuce, cheese slices, etc.)	

WHAT TO DO:

Cut the onion in half. Slice one half of the onion into rings and chop the other half into fine dice.

Place the minced beef, garlic, diced onion and seasonings in a bowl and mix really well to combine ingredients. Divide the mixture into 2 balls and flatten into patties. Refrigerate for ½ hour if you have time.

Heat the oil in the frying pan over a high heat and add the hamburgers and onion rings. Cook the hamburgers for about 3–5 minutes on each side until desired doneness. Stir the onions to ensure they are browned on all sides.

Remove the hamburgers from the frying pan and place on the buns, top with the onions, sauce of your choice and any other toppings.

Mince and Cabbage Bake

WHAT YOU'LL NEED:

Ingredients	Equipment
2 tablespoons oil	Stove top
250 g/9 oz lean minced beef	Oven
1 small onion, finely chopped	Saucepan
150 g/5 oz cabbage, thinly sliced	Ovenproof dish
1 clove garlic, finely chopped	Chopping board
1 tablespoon curry powder	Sharp knife
2 tablespoons tomato ketchup	Tablespoon
Salt and pepper	Cup
½ cup milk	
1 egg yolk	
150 g/5 oz cheese, grated	

WHAT TO DO:

Preheat the oven to 180°C/350°F/gas mark 4. Heat half the oil in a saucepan, add the minced meat and cook until the meat has turned brown, stirring constantly to break up any lumps. Remove and set aside.

Add the remaining oil to the saucepan then add the onion, cabbage and garlic and cook over a medium heat for about 10 minutes. Add the curry powder and tomato ketchup and cook for a couple of minutes.

Return the meat to the saucepan and add ½ cup water and salt and pepper to taste. Stir to combine and pour the mixture into a greased baking dish. Mix the milk, egg yolk and cheese in a bowl and pour over the meat mixture. Bake for 20 minutes.

Sausage Casserole

Serves 2

WHAT YOU'LL NEED:

Ingredients
2 tablespoons oil
3–4 sausages (depending on size)
1 onion, chopped
400 g/14 oz can chopped
  tomatoes
400 g/14 oz can haricot beans
  or drained baked beans
1 tablespoon dried Italian herbs

Equipment
Stove top
Large frying pan
Can opener
Chopping board
Sharp knife
Tablespoon

WHAT TO DO:

Heat half the oil in a frying pan and cook the sausages until cooked through.

Remove the sausages from the frying pan and cut each sausage into three pieces.

Add remaining oil to the frying pan and cook the onion for about 5 minutes or until tender, then add the chopped tomatoes, beans and herbs.

Return the sausages to the frying pan and simmer for about 15 minutes or until the mixture thickens. Stir occasionally to ensure the sauce doesn't stick to the bottom of the pan.

Serve with fresh bread.

Savoury Mince

Serves 2

WHAT YOU'LL NEED:

Ingredients
2 tablespoons olive oil
250 g/9 oz lean minced beef
1 small onion, finely chopped
1 carrot, finely chopped
1 stick celery, finely chopped
1 clove garlic, finely chopped
400 g/14 oz can chopped
  tomatoes
½ cup water
2 tablespoons curry powder
Salt and pepper

Equipment
Stove top
Large saucepan
Can opener
Chopping board
Sharp knife
Tablespoon
Cup

WHAT TO DO:

Heat the oil in a saucepan over a medium heat. Add the minced meat and cook until the meat has turned brown, stirring constantly to break up any lumps.

Add the onion, carrot, celery and garlic and cook gently for about 10 minutes.

Add the tomatoes, water and seasonings and simmer over a gentle heat, uncovered, for about 30 minutes or until the sauce thickens.

Serve with toast or crusty bread.

Greek Lamb Chops

Serves 2

WHAT YOU'LL NEED:

Ingredients
2 tablespoons olive oil
1 tablespoon fresh rosemary, finely chopped
1 clove garlic, finely chopped
Zest of 1 small lemon
Salt and pepper
4 lamb loin chops

Equipment
Stove top
Frying pan
Shallow dish or plate
Grater
Chopping board
Sharp knife
Tablespoon

WHAT TO DO:

Combine the olive oil, rosemary, garlic, lemon zest, salt and pepper in a shallow bowl or plate. Place the lamb chops into the mixture and turn over to coat both sides evenly. Cover the dish and set aside for about 15 minutes.

Place the frying pan on a high heat and, when the surface is hot, add the chops. Cook the chops for about 4 minutes then turn over and cook the other side for a further 4 minutes. Remove the chops from the frying pan and let them sit for a couple of minutes before serving.

Lamb and Feta Patties

Serves 2

WHAT YOU'LL NEED:

Ingredients
250 g/9 oz minced lamb
2 cloves garlic, finely chopped
50 g/2 oz feta cheese, crumbled
1 teaspoon dried Italian herbs
Salt and pepper
1 tablespoon olive oil

Equipment
Stove top
Large frying pan
Chopping board
Sharp knife
Tablespoon
Teaspoon
Bowl

WHAT TO DO:

Place the minced lamb, garlic, cheese, herbs, salt and pepper in a bowl and mix well to combine all the ingredients.

Divide the mixture into 4 balls and flatten into patties. Refrigerate for ½ hour if you have time.

Heat the oil in a frying pan over a high heat and add the patties. Cook the patties for about 4–5 minutes on each side.

Serve with pita bread and salad.

Pork Chops with Cider Sauce

Serves 2

WHAT YOU'LL NEED:

Ingredients
Salt and pepper
2 large pork chops
1 tablespoon olive oil
1 apple, sliced
125 ml/4 fl oz/½ cup cider
1 teaspoon sugar

Equipment
Stove top
Oven
Frying pan with lid
Baking tray
Chopping board
Sharp knife
Tablespoon
Teaspoon
Cup

WHAT TO DO:

Preheat the oven to 200°C/400°F/gas mark 6.

Sprinkle the salt and pepper onto the pork chops. Heat the oil in a frying pan, add the pork chops and cook for 2–3 minutes on each side until browned

Place the chops on the baking tray and bake for about 6 minutes or until they are cooked through.

Meanwhile, put the sliced apple and cider in the frying pan. Bring to the boil, cover and cook for 5 minutes or until the apple has softened. Add the sugar and stir until dissolved.

Take the pork chops out of the oven and serve with the sauce.

Moussaka

Serves 2

WHAT YOU'LL NEED:

Ingredients	Equipment
1 small aubergine/eggplant	Stove top
3 tablespoons olive oil	Oven
1 small onion, chopped	Large frying pan
1 garlic clove, crushed	Ovenproof dish
250 g/9 oz minced lamb (or beef)	Can opener
400 g/14 oz can chopped tomatoes	Small bowl
1 teaspoon dried Italian herbs	Grater
Salt and pepper	Chopping board
250 g/9 oz/1 cup ricotta cheese	Sharp knife
1 egg yolk	Tablespoon
75 g/3 oz/¾ cup cheese, grated	Teaspoon
	Cup

WHAT TO DO:

Preheat the oven to 200°C/400°F/gas mark 6.

Cut the aubergine/eggplant width wise into 1 cm/½ in slices. Heat 1 tablespoon oil in a frying pan over a high heat and cook the aubergine/eggplant slices until they are slightly charred on one side.

Add another tablespoon of oil, turn the aubergine/eggplant over and cook on the other side until browned. Remove and set aside.

Pour the remaining oil into the frying pan over a medium heat and add the onion, garlic and minced meat. Cook for about 10 minutes until the meat is browned, stirring to break up lumps and prevent sticking.

Add the tomatoes, herbs, salt and pepper and simmer for about 10 minutes.

Layer the aubergine/eggplant slices along the bottom of a baking dish and pour the meat and tomato mixture over the top.

Place the ricotta cheese, egg yolk and half the cheese in a bowl and mix thoroughly.

Pour the cheese over the meat mixture and spread evenly to the edges. Sprinkle with the remaining grated cheese.

Bake for about 20 minutes or until the top has browned.

Pork with Mushrooms and Wine

Serves 2

WHAT YOU'LL NEED:

Ingredients
2 tablespoons oil
1 small onion, finely chopped
1 cup mushrooms, sliced
2 cloves garlic, crushed
250 g/9 oz pork fillets, cut into
 1.5 cm/⅔ in slices
65 ml/2 fl oz/¼ cup white wine
65 ml/2 fl oz/¼ cup cream
1 tablespoon fresh sage, chopped
 (or 1 teaspoon dried Italian herbs)
Salt and pepper

Equipment
Stove top
Saucepan with lid
Chopping board
Sharp knife
Tablespoon
Cup

WHAT TO DO:

Heat the oil in a saucepan, add the onion and cook for about
5 minutes. Add the mushrooms and garlic and cook for a further
3 minutes.

Add the pork and cook for 3–5 minutes until it is golden brown.

Pour in the wine and cream and add the seasonings. Put the lid on
the saucepan and simmer gently for about 10 minutes or until the
pork is cooked through.

Serve with mashed potato, rice or noodles.

Fish Dishes

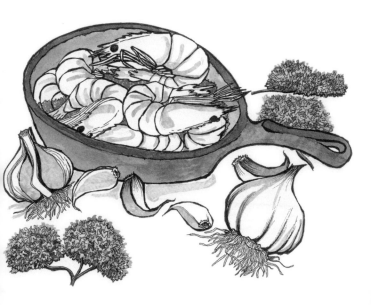

Garlic and Lemon Prawns see page 86

How to Cook Fish

The amount of time needed to cook fresh fish will greatly depend on the type of fish you choose and the thickness of the fillet or steak. Ideally, you're looking to cook the fish right through but not overcook it so that it becomes too dry.

An easy way to cook fish is to wrap it in aluminium foil with a splash of olive oil and fresh lemon juice and bake it for approximately 15 minutes on a high heat (200°C/400°F/gas mark 6). You can also pan fry fish on a medium heat for around 5 minutes on each side, or place under a grill for the same amount of time.

When using canned fish, such as salmon or tuna, the fish has already been cooked, so you only really need to warm it through.

If you're going to buy prawns to cook in these recipes you should get raw prawns that are green in colour and turn pink once they're cooked through. If you use pre-cooked prawns they will only need to be warmed through and will not absorb any additional flavours. Precooked prawns are great to buy and eat naturally or with a squeeze of lemon juice.

Baked Fish and Asparagus Parcels   Serves 2

WHAT YOU'LL NEED:

Ingredients	Equipment
12 asparagus spears	Oven
2 fish fillets (meaty white fish like cod)	Chopping board
	Sharp knife
25 g/1 oz chopped butter	Grater
Chilli flakes (optional)	Aluminium foil
1 lemon, zest and juice	

WHAT TO DO:

Preheat the oven to 200°C/400°F/gas mark 6.

Take two 30 cm/12 in squares of foil and divide the asparagus between them. Make sure you snap the woody ends off the asparagus first.

Cut the fish into cubes and place on top of the asparagus. Place the butter, chilli flakes and lemon onto the fish, then fold up the parcels so that they are properly sealed.

Place the parcels onto a baking tray and bake for 15–18 minutes.

Baked Fish with Tomato and Thyme   Serves 2

WHAT YOU'LL NEED:

Ingredients	Equipment
1 tablespoon oil	Stove top
½ onion, chopped	Frying pan with lid
400 g/14 oz can	Can opener
chopped tomatoes	Chopping board
1 tablespoon sugar	Sharp knife
Few sprigs fresh thyme	Tablespoon
2 cod fillets (or other meaty	
white fish)	

WHAT TO DO:

Heat the oil in a frying pan and add the onion. Cook for a few minutes until the onion has softened.

Add the tomatoes, sugar and thyme and bring to the boil. Reduce the heat and simmer for 5 minutes.

Place the cod into the sauce, cover the frying pan with a lid and cook on a low heat for 8–10 minutes.

Baked Salmon and Crushed Peas   Serves 2

WHAT YOU'LL NEED:

Ingredients	Equipment
2 salmon fillets	Stove top
2 tablespoons oil	Oven
2 spring onions, sliced	Ovenproof dish
1 clove garlic, finely chopped	Small saucepan
250 ml/8 fl oz/1 cup chicken stock	Chopping board
1 cup frozen peas	Sharp knife
1 teaspoon sugar	Cup
¼ cup mint leaves, chopped	Tablespoon
	Teaspoon

WHAT TO DO:

Preheat the oven to 140°C/275°F/gas mark 1.

Place the salmon in an ovenproof dish and drizzle half the oil over it. Bake the fish for 15 minutes or until just cooked through.

Heat the remaining oil in the saucepan, add the spring onions and cook gently for a few minutes. Add the garlic, stock, peas and sugar and cook gently for about 10 minutes. Remove from the heat, crush the peas with a fork, add the mint and stir well.

Place the salmon on 2 plates, pour over the crushed peas and serve with mashed potato.

Fish Cakes

Serves 2

WHAT YOU'LL NEED:

Ingredients

2 medium potatoes,
  peeled and quartered
185 g/6½ oz can pink salmon
  or tuna
1 egg yolk
1 small onion, finely chopped
1 tablespoon parsley, finely chopped
2 tablespoons oil
Salt and pepper

Equipment

Stove top
Frying pan
Can opener
Bowl
Chopping board
Sharp knife
Tablespoon

WHAT TO DO:

Boil the potatoes until tender and mash until smooth.

Drain the salmon/tuna and remove any bones. Combine all the
ingredients in a bowl and refrigerate for 15 minutes. Divide the
mixture into 4 balls and flatten into patties. Refrigerate for a further
15 minutes if you have time.

Heat the oil in a frying pan over a low–medium heat. Add the fish
cakes and cook for about 5 minutes on each side.

Fish Stew

WHAT YOU'LL NEED:

Ingredients	Equipment
1 tablespoon olive oil	Stove top
1 small onion, chopped	Large frying pan
1 clove garlic, finely chopped	Chopping board
400 g/14 oz can chopped tomatoes	Sharp knife
125 ml/4 fl oz/½ cup water	Cup
1 tablespoon capers, drained	Tablespoon
12 pitted black olives	
Salt and pepper	
2 thick/firm white fish fillets	
(approximately 180 g/6 oz each)	
2 tablespoons freshly sliced basil	

WHAT TO DO:

Heat the oil in a frying pan and cook the onion for 5 minutes, add the garlic and cook for a further 2 minutes.

Add the tomatoes, water, capers, olives and seasoning and stir well. Bring to the boil then lower the heat and cook gently for 10 minutes.

Cut the fish fillets into chunks and add to the sauce along with the basil. Mix well and simmer for about 5 minutes until the fish is just cooked (the fish should turn from opaque to white). Add more water as required.

Poached Salmon Fillets

Serves 2

WHAT YOU'LL NEED:

Ingredients	Equipment
125 ml/4 fl oz/½ cup dry white wine	Stove top
125 ml/4 fl oz/½ cup water	Frying pan with lid
½ onion, sliced	Chopping board
250 g/9 oz salmon fillet, cut into two pieces	Sharp knife
	Cup

WHAT TO DO:

Pour the wine and water into the frying pan, add the onion and bring to the boil.

Reduce the heat to medium and place the salmon fillets in the liquid skin-side down.

Cover the frying pan and cook the salmon for 7–10 minutes until it changes colour and becomes opaque.

Salmon and Corn Bake

Serves 2

WHAT YOU'LL NEED:

Ingredients
1 small courgette/zucchini, grated
185 g/6½ oz can pink salmon,
  drained
2 eggs
2 tablespoons plain flour
200 g/7 oz can creamed corn
50 g/2 oz/½ cup cheese, grated
¼ teaspoon dried Italian herbs

Equipment
Oven
Ovenproof dish
Can opener
Grater
Tablespoon
Teaspoon
Cup

WHAT TO DO:

Preheat the oven to 180°C/350°F/gas mark 4.

Squeeze the grated courgette/zucchini with your hands until most of the moisture has been removed.

Drain the salmon and remove any bones.

Beat the eggs and flour until smooth. Add the remaining ingredients and mix well until combined. Pour the mixture into a greased baking dish.

Bake for 30–40 minutes.

Tuna Slice

Serves 2

WHAT YOU'LL NEED:

Ingredients	Equipment
185 g/6½ oz can tuna, drained	Oven
75 g/3 oz/¾ cup cheese, grated	Ovenproof dish
½ cup savoury biscuits, crushed	Can opener
1 egg, beaten	Chopping board
½ cup milk	Sharp knife
1 small onion, finely chopped	Cup
Pepper	Grater
Oil or butter to grease dish	

WHAT TO DO:

Preheat the oven to 200°C/400°F/gas mark 6.

Drain the tuna and remove any bones.

Place all the ingredients (reserving 2 tablespoons cheese) in a bowl and mix thoroughly. Pour the mixture into a well greased ovenproof dish, sprinkle with extra cheese and press down.

Bake for 30–40 minutes or until golden on top. Serve hot or cold.

Creole Prawns

Serves 2

WHAT YOU'LL NEED:

Ingredients

1 tablespoon olive oil
1 onion, finely chopped
1 garlic clove, finely chopped
1 green pepper, finely chopped
12 raw/green king prawns, peeled
400 g/14 oz can chopped tomatoes
   or passata
1 teaspoon chilli flakes

Equipment

Stove top
Frying pan
Chopping board
Sharp knife

WHAT TO DO:

Heat the oil in a frying pan and add the onion, garlic and pepper.
Cook for 5 minutes until softened.

Add the raw prawns and cook for 5 minutes until they start
to turn pink.

Stir in the tomatoes and chilli flakes and bring to the boil.
Turn the heat down and simmer for a further 3–5 minutes.

Serve with rice or pasta.

Garlic and Lemon Prawns

Serves 2

WHAT YOU'LL NEED:

Ingredients	Equipment
1 tablespoon olive oil	Stove top
12 raw/green king prawns	Frying pan
Splash of white wine	Chopping board
3 garlic cloves, finely chopped	Sharp knife
1 lemon, zest and juice	Grater
¼ cup fresh parsley, chopped	Cup

WHAT TO DO:

Heat the oil in a frying pan and add the prawns. When they start to turn pink, add the white wine. Turn the heat down and then add the garlic. Add the lemon zest and juice and simmer for a few minutes until the liquid reduces.

Stir in the parsley just before serving with salad and crusty bread.

Pasta and Rice Dishes

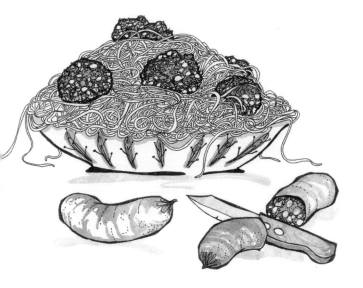

Spaghetti with Meatballs see page 98

How to Cook Pasta and Rice

Most packets of dried pasta and rice will come with their own cooking instructions but, if not, or you don't understand the language, there are a few basic rules of thumb to guarantee the best results.

PASTA

Fill a large saucepan with water so that it's around 2 inches from the top and bring to the boil. When it's boiling, add a dash of olive oil and a pinch of salt if you have them. Add the amount of pasta you wish to eat (approximately 100 g/4 oz per person) and stir it in to the water. Once the cooking time has passed (approximately 12 minutes for dried pasta or 3–5 minutes if you're lucky enough to get fresh pasta) test a piece – ideally it should be al dente, which means that it's still slightly firm and not mushy soft. Drain the water out of the pan and add your sauce.

RICE (LONG GRAIN)

Always try to rinse your rice before cooking it to remove any excess starch and keep the grains separate. Fill your saucepan with water as with the pasta and add a pinch of salt if you have it. Once the water is boiling, add the rice (approximately ½ cup per person) and stir. Test the rice a few minutes before it's due to be ready (after approximately 12 minutes) and then drain the water out of the pan. Rice can also be cooked in a microwave by putting one cup of rice and two cups of boiling water in a microwave-proof dish, covering and cooking for approximately 12–13 minutes on high.

RICE (SHORT GRAIN)

Short grain rice is used in dishes where a creamy texture is required. To make risotto you need a short grain rice which absorbs large amounts of liquid (usually stock) and releases starch with frequent stirring; this gives it its beautiful velvety consistency. It can take up to 30 minutes to cook risotto using the conventional method on the stove top. Arborio is a popular and cheap version of this rice but any short grain rice can be used.

Macaroni Cheese

Serves 2

WHAT YOU'LL NEED:

Ingredients
200 g/7 oz macaroni
150 g/5 oz/1½ cups (firmly packed)
  cheddar cheese, grated
190 ml/6 fl oz/¾ cup cream
Pepper

Equipment
Stove top
Large saucepan
Grater
Cup

WHAT TO DO:

Cook the macaroni in a large pan of boiling water according to packet instructions. When al dente, drain the macaroni and return to the pan.

Add the cheese, cream and pepper and stir over a low heat until the cheese has melted and the sauce has thickened.

Note: For a more substantial dish you can add 2 diced and cooked bacon rashers.

Pasta Aglio e Olio (Garlic and Olive Oil)

Serves 2

WHAT YOU'LL NEED:

Ingredients	Equipment
65 g/3 oz/¼ cup olive oil (extra virgin if possible)	Stove top
	Large saucepan
4 cloves garlic, crushed	Large frying pan
1 teaspoon chilli flakes (optional)	Grater
1 tablespoon parsley, finely chopped	Chopping board
Salt and pepper	Sharp knife
200 g/7 oz pasta of your choice	Tablespoon
25 g/1 oz/¼ cup parmesan cheese, grated	Teaspoon

WHAT TO DO:

Heat the oil in a frying pan and add the garlic. When the garlic starts to brown, add the chilli flakes, parsley, salt and pepper. Remove from the heat and stir well.

Meanwhile, cook the pasta in a large pan of boiling water according to the packet instructions. When al dente, drain.

Add the cooked pasta to the frying pan and mix thoroughly to ensure the flavoured oil coats all of the pasta. Sprinkle with the parmesan cheese before serving.

Pasta Bolognaise

Serves 2

WHAT YOU'LL NEED:

Ingredients	Equipment
2 tablespoons olive oil	Stove top
200 g/7 oz lean minced beef	Large saucepan
1 small onion, finely chopped	Can opener
1 clove garlic, finely chopped	Grater
400 g/14 oz can	Chopping board
tomato purée/passata	Sharp knife
1 teaspoon dried Italian herbs	Teaspoon
Salt and pepper	Tablespoon
200 g/7 oz pasta of your choice	
25 g/1 oz/¼ cup parmesan	
cheese, grated	

WHAT TO DO:

Heat the oil in a saucepan over a medium heat. Add the minced meat and cook until the meat has turned brown, stirring constantly to break up any lumps. Add the onion and garlic and cook gently for about 10 minutes.

Add the tomato purée/passata, half a can of water and seasonings and simmer over a gentle heat, uncovered, for about 30 minutes or until the sauce thickens.

Meanwhile, cook the pasta in a large pan of boiling water according to the packet instructions. When al dente, drain and transfer to plates. Ladle the sauce over the pasta and sprinkle with parmesan cheese before serving.

Pasta Carbonara

Serves 2

WHAT YOU'LL NEED:

Ingredients	Equipment
1 tablespoon oil	Stove top
2 bacon rashers, chopped	Large saucepan
3 eggs	Large frying pan
65 g/3 oz/¼ cup cream	Small bowl
50 g/2 oz/½ cup parmesan	Grater
cheese, grated	Chopping board
Pepper	Sharp knife
200 g/7 oz pasta of your choice	Tablespoon

WHAT TO DO:

Heat the oil in a frying pan and cook the bacon on a high heat until crisp.

Combine the eggs, cream, cheese (reserve 2 tablespoons) and pepper in a bowl and mix well.

Meanwhile, cook the pasta in a large pan of boiling water according to the packet instructions. When al dente, drain and add to the frying pan along with the egg mixture. Toss over a low heat until the sauce coats the pasta and thickens slightly. Be careful not to overcook.

Transfer the pasta to plates and scatter the remaining cheese over the top before serving.

Pasta Puttanesca

Serves 2

WHAT YOU'LL NEED:

Ingredients
2 tablespoons olive oil
1 small onion, finely chopped
2 anchovy fillets, chopped (optional)
4 tomatoes, chopped
1 tablespoon black olives, pitted
  and chopped
1 tablespoon capers, drained
1 clove garlic, finely chopped
½ chilli, deseeded and finely chopped
200 g/7 oz pasta of your choice
1 tablespoon parsley, chopped

Equipment
Stove top
Large frying pan
Large saucepan
Chopping board
Sharp knife
Tablespoon

WHAT TO DO:

Heat the oil in a frying pan over a medium heat. Add the onion (and anchovy if using) and cook for about 5 minutes. Add the tomatoes, olives, capers, garlic and chilli and cook for a further 10 minutes.

Meanwhile, cook the pasta in a large pan of boiling water according to the packet instructions. When al dente, drain and toss the sauce through the pasta.

Sprinkle with parsley before serving.

Pasta with Lemon and Basil

Serves 2

WHAT YOU'LL NEED:

Ingredients

¼ cup olive oil (preferably extra virgin)
50 g/2 oz/½ cup parmesan cheese, grated
Juice of 1 lemon (about ¼ cup)
1 teaspoon lemon zest
200 g/7 oz pasta of your choice
Small handful fresh basil, finely sliced
Salt and pepper

Equipment

Stove top
Large saucepan
Bowl
Grater
Chopping board
Sharp knife
Cup

WHAT TO DO:

Whisk the oil, parmesan cheese (reserve 2 tablespoons), lemon juice and zest in a bowl.

Meanwhile, cook the pasta in a large pan of boiling water according to the packet instructions. When al dente, drain the pasta and reserve ¼ cup of the liquid.

Return the pasta to the saucepan and add the sauce, water and basil. Season with salt and pepper and mix thoroughly to ensure the sauce coats all of the pasta.

Sprinkle with the reserved parmesan cheese before serving.

Pasta with Salami and Mushrooms   Serves 2

WHAT YOU'LL NEED:

Ingredients	Equipment
6 slices of salami, cut into strips	Stove top
8 mushrooms, peeled and sliced	Large saucepan
2 tablespoons of mascarpone cheese or crème fraiche	Medium saucepan or frying pan
3 tablespoons water	Grater
200 g/7 oz pasta of your choice	Chopping board
25 g/1 oz/¼ cup parmesan cheese, grated	Sharp knife
	Tablespoon

WHAT TO DO:

Place a saucepan on a medium heat and add the salami. Fry for 5 minutes or until the salami is crisp. Remove the salami and set aside, leaving the fat in the saucepan.

Add the mushrooms to the saucepan and cook over a medium heat for 5 minutes or until browned. Add the mascarpone cheese and water to the saucepan and cook gently until the sauce is thick and smooth.

Meanwhile, cook the pasta in a large pan of boiling water according to the packet instructions. When al dente, drain and toss sauce through the pasta. Add the salami and sprinkle with the parmesan cheese before serving.

Pasta with Tuna and Tomatoes

Serves 2

WHAT YOU'LL NEED:

Ingredients	Equipment
1 tablespoon olive oil	Stove top
1 small onion, finely chopped	Large saucepan
1 clove garlic, finely chopped	Large frying pan
185 g/6½ oz can tuna in oil	Can opener
400 g/14 oz can chopped	Chopping board
tomatoes	Sharp knife
1 tablespoon parsley,	Tablespoon
finely chopped	
200 g/7 oz pasta of your choice	

WHAT TO DO:

Heat the oil in a frying pan and cook the onion until soft. Add the garlic and cook for a further 1–2 minutes.

Add the tuna and tomatoes, bring to the boil and simmer over a gentle heat for 10 minutes. Remove from heat and stir in parsley.

Meanwhile, cook the pasta in a large pan of boiling water according to the packet instructions. When al dente, drain and toss the sauce through the pasta and serve.

Spaghetti with Meatballs

Serves 2

WHAT YOU'LL NEED:

Ingredients

4 Italian–style sausages
2 tablespoons olive oil
1 small onion, finely chopped
1 clove garlic, finely chopped
400 g/14 oz can tomato purée/passata
Salt and pepper
200 g/7 oz spaghetti
25 g/1 oz/¼ cup parmesan
  cheese, grated

Equipment

Stove top
Large frying pan
Large saucepan
Can opener
Grater
Chopping board
Sharp knife
Tablespoon

WHAT TO DO:

Cut the sausages in half and squeeze the meat out of the skins.
With wet hands roll the meat into balls, place on a plate and
refrigerate for 10 minutes.

Heat half the oil in a frying pan over a medium heat and cook the
meatballs for about 10 minutes, moving them around so they brown
evenly all over. Remove to a plate and keep warm.

Heat the remaining oil in the frying pan and cook the onion for
10 minutes. Add the garlic, tomato purée/passata and seasoning
and simmer for 15 minutes. Gently add the meatballs to the tomato
sauce and cook over a low heat for 5 minutes.

Meanwhile, cook the spaghetti in a large pan of boiling water
according to the packet instructions. When al dente, drain and
transfer to plates. Ladle the meatballs and sauce over the spaghetti
and sprinkle with parmesan cheese before serving.

Budget Paella

Serves 2

WHAT YOU'LL NEED:

Ingredients	Equipment
1 tablespoon olive oil	Stove top
50 g/2 oz chorizo, cut into 1 cm/½ in pieces	Large frying pan with lid
1 small onion, chopped	Chopping board
1 red pepper, chopped	Sharp knife
1 chilli, deseeded and finely chopped	Tablespoon
1 clove garlic, finely chopped	Cup
2 tomatoes, chopped	
2 chicken thighs, cut into 2 cm/¾ in pieces	
110 g/4 oz/½ cup long grain rice	
250 ml/8 fl oz/1 cup chicken stock	
4 raw/green king prawns, peeled	
½ cup frozen peas	

WHAT TO DO:

Heat the oil in a frying pan and cook the chorizo for 3 minutes. Add the onion, pepper, chilli and garlic and cook for a further 5 minutes.

Add the tomatoes, chicken pieces, rice and stock and bring to the boil. Cover the frying pan, lower the heat and simmer gently for about 10 minutes.

Add the prawns and peas and cook for 5 minutes or until the chicken is cooked through and the prawns have turned pink.

Fried Rice

Serves 2

WHAT YOU'LL NEED:

Ingredients
110 g/4 oz/½ cup long
   grain/basmati rice
2 eggs
2 tablespoons oil
2 bacon rashers, chopped
1 clove garlic, finely chopped
2 spring onions, thinly sliced
½ cup bean sprouts
1 tablespoon soy sauce,
   plus extra to serve

Equipment
Stove top
Large saucepan
Large frying pan
Tablespoon

WHAT TO DO:

Cook the rice in a large saucepan of boiling water for about
12 minutes or until tender. Drain the rice and rinse under cold
water to remove the starch. Spread out on a plate and place in the
refrigerator to cool.

Place the eggs in a small bowl and whisk until frothy. Heat half the
oil in a frying pan over a medium heat. Add the eggs and swirl them
around the base of the pan to make a sort of pancake. Cook for
about 2 minutes, then turn over and cook the other side for a further
2 minutes or until set. Transfer the egg pancake to a chopping board,
allow to cool slightly and cut into short strips.

Add the remaining oil to the frying pan and cook the bacon on a high
heat until crisp. Add the cold rice and cook, stirring, until warmed
through. Add the garlic, egg strips, spring onions, bean sprouts and
soy sauce. Stir for 2 minutes then serve immediately with extra soy.

Kedgeree

Serves 2

WHAT YOU'LL NEED:

Ingredients	Equipment
165 g/6 oz/¾ cup long grain/basmati rice	Stove top
185 g/6½ oz pink salmon, drained	Large saucepan
2 eggs	Chopping board
2 tablespoons butter	Sharp knife
2 spring onions, sliced	Tablespoon
1 tablespoon curry powder	
Juice of 1 lemon	
¼ cup parsley, chopped	

WHAT TO DO:

Cook the rice in a saucepan of boiling water for about 12 minutes or until tender. Drain the rice and rinse under cold water to remove the starch. Spread out on a plate and place in the refrigerator to cool. Drain the salmon and remove any bones.

Boil the eggs for about 7 minutes, plunge into cold water and, when cool enough to handle, peel and cut into quarters.

Melt the butter in the saucepan and add the spring onions. Cook for 2 minutes before adding the curry powder. Cook for a further 2 minutes, then add the lemon juice, rice and salmon and gently warm through.

Add the eggs and parsley, stir gently and serve.

Moroccan Rice

Serves 2

WHAT YOU'LL NEED:

Ingredients
2 chicken breasts, cut into
  2 cm/¾ in pieces
1 tablespoon Moroccan spice
1 tablespoon olive oil
½ onion, finely sliced
110 g/4 oz/½ cup long
  grain/basmati rice
6 dried apricots
200 g/7 oz can chickpeas, drained
250 ml/8 fl oz/1 cup chicken stock
Handful fresh parsley, chopped

Equipment
Stove top
Large frying pan with lid
Chopping board
Sharp knife
Tablespoon
Cup

WHAT TO DO:

Coat the chicken in the Moroccan spice and set aside.

Heat the oil in a frying pan and add the onion. Cook for a few minutes until the onion has softened. Add the chicken and cook for 3–4 minutes.

Add the rice, apricots, chickpeas and stock.

Cover the frying pan and simmer on a low heat for about 10 minutes until the rice is tender and has absorbed most of the liquid.

Sprinkle with chopped parsley and serve.

Thai Chicken Coconut Rice

WHAT YOU'LL NEED:

Ingredients
1 tablespoon oil
½ onion chopped
2 chicken breasts, cut into
   1.5 cm/⅔ in strips
2 tablespoons Thai green chicken
   curry paste
220 g/8 oz/1 cup long
   grain/basmati rice
1 red pepper, sliced
Juice of ½ lime
400 g/14 oz tin coconut milk
125 ml/4 fl oz/½ cup boiling water
Handful fresh coriander leaves, chopped

Equipment
Oven
Stove top
Saucepan
Baking dish
Chopping board
Sharp knife

WHAT TO DO:
Preheat the oven to 180°C/350°F/gas mark 4.

Heat the oil in a saucepan and add the onion. Cook for a few minutes until the onion has softened.

Add the chicken and curry paste and cook for 3 minutes, stirring to make sure the chicken is coated in the sauce.

Stir in the rice, pepper, lime juice, coconut milk and boiling water. Bring to the boil and pour the mixture into an ovenproof dish.

Bake for 20 minutes or until the rice is cooked. Sprinkle with coriander and serve.

Risotto

Serves 2

WHAT YOU'LL NEED:

Ingredients	Equipment
1 tablespoon olive oil	Stove top
1 onion, finely chopped	Saucepan
220 g/8 oz/1 cup short grain (arborio) rice	Chopping board
	Sharp knife
500 ml/17 fl oz/2 cups boiling chicken stock	Tablespoon
	Cup
Flavouring of your choice	Bowl
Handful fresh parmesan cheese, grated	
1 tablespoon butter	

WHAT TO DO:

Heat the oil in a large frying pan and add the onion. Cook over a medium heat for around 3 minutes until the onion has softened. Add the rice and cook for a further 2 minutes, stirring to coat the rice in the oil.

Bring the stock to the boil in another saucepan and start adding some liquid (about ¼ cup at a time) to the rice, stirring regularly. Wait until the rice absorbs the liquid before adding more.

Once the rice has absorbed all of the stock (this could take around 25 minutes) and is cooked through, take the saucepan off the heat and add the flavouring of your choice (see below).

Just before serving, add a handful of freshly grated parmesan cheese and a knob of butter. Mix through and serve.

Note: Always cook your flavourings first and then put to the side while the rice is cooking. You need to add them at the last minute to retain their flavour.

Combinations to try include:

Chicken and mushroom
Cut 1 chicken breast into 2 cm/¾ in pieces and fry in a small amount of oil for 3–4 minutes until cooked through. Remove from the pan and add ½ cup sliced mushrooms, then cook for 3–4 minutes until brown. When the rice is cooked, add the chicken and mushrooms as well and the liquid from the pan to the risotto mixture and stir through.

Pea, mint and prawn
Shell 1 cup of uncooked prawns and fry over a medium heat for 1–2 minutes or until they turn pink. When the rice is cooked, add the prawns, ½ cup of frozen peas and a handful of chopped fresh mint to the risotto mixture. Stir through until the peas are soft.

Courgette/zucchini and bacon
Chop 2 rashers of bacon and 1 courgette/zucchini into bitesized pieces then fry over a medium heat for 3–4 minutes or until the bacon is crispy. When the rice is cooked, add the courgette/zucchini and bacon to the risotto mixture.

Vegetarian Dishes

Spanish Baked Eggs see page 116

Baked Mushrooms

Serves 2

WHAT YOU'LL NEED:

Ingredients
6 large mushrooms
  (stalks removed)
2 large tomatoes, sliced
2 tablespoons pesto or handful
  fresh basil
50 g/2 oz mozzarella cheese,
  sliced or grated

Equipment
Oven
Baking tray
Chopping board
Sharp knife

WHAT TO DO:
Preheat the oven to 200°C/400°F/gas mark 6.

Place the mushrooms on a baking tray. Layer two slices of tomato on each mushroom and add the pesto or torn basil.

Bake the mushrooms for 10 minutes. Remove from the oven, top with the cheese and return to the oven for a further 10 minutes or until the cheese has melted.

Bubble and Squeak Patties

Serves 2

WHAT YOU'LL NEED:

Ingredients
2 large potatoes, peeled
   and quartered
2 tablespoons oil
1 small onion, finely chopped
1 cup cabbage, thinly sliced
Salt and pepper

Equipment
Stove
Large saucepan
Frying pan (preferably non-stick)
Chopping board
Sharp knife
Tablespoon
Cup

WHAT TO DO:

Cook the potatoes in boiling water until tender, drain and mash.

Heat half the oil in a frying pan and cook the onion over a medium heat for about 5 minutes. Add the cabbage and cook gently for another 5 minutes or until tender. Add a little water if the vegetables are starting to burn on the bottom of the pan.

Mix the mashed potato and fried vegetables together. Divide the mixture into 4 balls and flatten into patties. Refrigerate for ½ hour if you have time.

Heat the remaining oil in a frying pan over a medium heat. Add the patties and cook for about 5 minutes on each side.

Couscous and Roasted Vegetables   Serves 2

WHAT YOU'LL NEED:

Ingredients	Equipment
125 ml/4 fl oz/½ cup chicken stock	Stove top
140 g/5 oz/½ cup couscous	Oven
Salt and pepper	Small saucepan
1 tablespoon dried Italian herbs	Ovenproof dish
1 tablespoon lemon juice	Chopping board
3 tablespoons olive oil	Sharp knife
1 red pepper	Tablespoon
1 courgette/zucchini	Cup
1 small onion	
8 cherry tomatoes	
1 clove garlic, sliced	

WHAT TO DO:

Preheat the oven to 180°C/350°F/gas mark 4.

Bring the stock to the boil then remove from the heat. Add the couscous, cover and set aside for 5 minutes. Stir with a fork to fluff up and separate the grains. Add the seasoning, lemon juice and 1 tablespoon of oil.

Cut the vegetables into similar sized pieces (approximately 2.5 cm/1in square) and place them with the garlic in a baking dish. Pour over the remaining oil and sprinkle with seasonings.

Bake the vegetables for about 20–30 minutes, stirring regularly, until browned and tender. To serve, place a mound of couscous on each plate and top with roasted vegetables.

Frittata

Serves 2

WHAT YOU'LL NEED:

Ingredients	Equipment
1 tablespoon oil	Stove top
2 large potatoes, peeled and chopped into 1.5 cm/⅔ in pieces	Oven
	Ovenproof frying pan
1 small onion, chopped	Small bowl
6 eggs	Chopping board
4 tablespoons milk	Sharp knife
Salt and pepper	Tablespoon

WHAT TO DO:

Preheat the oven to 200°C/400°F/gas mark 6.

Heat the oil in a frying pan over a low–medium heat. Add the potato and onion and cook until the potato is softened but not falling apart.

Place the eggs, milk and seasoning in a bowl and whisk until combined. Pour the mixture over the potatoes and onion and transfer to the oven. Bake until the egg mixture is browned on top and set in the middle.

Note: For variety you can add ½ cup sliced mushrooms to the potato and onion mixture when cooking, or ½ cup grated cheddar cheese or ½ cup thinly sliced spinach to the egg mixture. Just use your imagination.

Spicy Dahl

Serves 2

WHAT YOU'LL NEED:

Ingredients	Equipment
1 tablespoon olive oil	Stove top
1 onion, finely chopped	Saucepan
1 clove garlic, crushed	Chopping board
2 cm/¾ in piece fresh ginger, finely chopped	Sharp knife
1 tablespoon curry powder	Tablespoon
1 lt/32 fl oz/4 cups water	Cup
200 g/7 oz/1 cup red lentils	

WHAT TO DO:

Heat the oil in a saucepan, add the onion and cook until browned. Add the garlic, ginger and curry powder and fry for about a minute, or until you can smell the powder cooking.

Add the water and lentils and bring to the boil. Cook on a high heat until almost all of the liquid has absorbed (around 20–25 minutes), stirring occasionally.

Spinach and Mushroom Soufflé Omelette

Serves 2

WHAT YOU'LL NEED:

Ingredients	Equipment
2 tablespoons butter	Stove top
½ cup mushrooms, chopped	Frying pan
4 medium eggs	Chopping board
½ cup baby leaf spinach	Sharp knife
100 g/4 oz feta cheese, chopped	2 bowls

WHAT TO DO:

Heat half the butter in a frying pan and add the mushrooms. Cook for 3 minutes until the mushrooms have turned brown.

Separate the eggs and place the yolks in one bowl and the whites in another. Add the spinach, cheese and cooked mushrooms to the egg yolks and mix well.

In the other bowl, whisk the egg whites with a fork until bubbles appear on the surface. Gently fold the whites into the cheese and mushroom mixture.

Melt the remaining butter in a frying pan and pour in the mixture. Cook for 3–5 minutes until golden on the underside. Fold the omelette in half and cook for a further couple of minutes until the centre is cooked through.

Tofu Provencal

WHAT YOU'LL NEED:

Ingredients	Equipment
250 g/9 oz firm tofu	Stove top
2 tablespoons olive oil	Large frying pan
1 small onion, finely chopped	Can opener
2 cloves garlic, finely chopped	Chopping board
400 g/14 oz can chopped	Sharp knife
tomatoes	Tablespoon
1 teaspoon dried Italian herbs	Teaspoon
Salt and pepper	
2 tablespoons black olives,	
pitted and chopped	

WHAT TO DO:

Pat tofu dry and cut into 1.5 cm/^{2}/$_3$ in cubes. Heat half the oil in a frying pan, add the tofu and cook over a medium–high heat until golden brown. Remove from the pan and set aside.

Pour the remaining oil into the frying pan, add the onion and garlic and cook for 5 minutes. Add the tomatoes, herbs, salt and pepper and simmer for about 15 minutes until the sauce has reduced and thickened.

Return the tofu to the pan, add the olives and seasonings and cook gently until warmed through.

Vegetarian Moussaka

Serves 2

WHAT YOU'LL NEED:

Ingredients	Equipment
1 aubergine/eggplant	Oven hob
1 tablespoon olive oil	Frying pan
1 tablespoon dried Italian herbs	Ovenproof dish
400 g/14 oz can chopped	Chopping board
tomatoes	Sharp knife
50 g/2 oz mozzarella, thinly sliced	

WHAT TO DO:

Preheat the oven to 200°C/400°F/gas mark 6.

Cut the aubergine/eggplant width-wise into 1 cm/½ in slices.
Heat the oil in a frying pan over a high heat and cook the
aubergine/eggplant slices until slightly charred. Remove and set aside.

Layer half the aubergine/eggplant slices along the bottom of a baking
dish. Add the Italian herbs to the can of tomatoes and pour half the
tomatoes over the aubergine/eggplant slices. Repeat layers.

Place the slices of mozzarella across the top of the dish.

Bake for 20 minutes.

Courgette/Zucchini Fritters

Serves 2

WHAT YOU'LL NEED:

Ingredients	Equipment
2 medium courgette/zucchini, coarsely grated	Stove top
1 clove garlic, finely chopped	Large frying pan
1 small onion, grated	Grater
50 g/2 oz/½ cup parmesan cheese, grated	Cup
Zest of half a lemon	Tablespoon
2 tablespoons oil	

WHAT TO DO:

Squeeze the grated courgette/zucchini with your hands until most of the moisture has been removed. Place all the ingredients (reserving half the oil) in a bowl and mix well.

Form the mixture into fritters. Refrigerate for ½ hour if you have time.

Heat the remaining oil in a frying pan over a medium heat. Add the fritters and cook for about 5 minutes on each side.

Spanish Baked Eggs

Serves 2

WHAT YOU'LL NEED:

Ingredients	Equipment
1 tablespoon olive oil	Stove top
1 red onion, chopped	Oven
1 garlic clove, crushed	Frying pan
1 green pepper, chopped	Ovenproof dish
400 g/14 oz can chopped	Can opener
tomatoes	Chopping board
4 eggs	Sharp knife
	Tablespoon

WHAT TO DO:

Preheat the oven to 200°C/400°F/gas mark 6.

Heat the oil in a frying pan and add the onion and garlic. Cook for 5 minutes until the onion has softened. Add the pepper and cook for 2–3 minutes before adding the tomatoes.

Pour the mixture into an ovenproof dish and make four hollows in the tomato and vegetable mixture. Break an egg into each hollow.

Bake for 10 minutes or until the egg whites set.

Vegetables and Salads

Greek Salad see page 121

How to Cook Vegetables

Listed below is a summary of the different types of vegetables, and the most suitable cooking methods.

Family	Vegetables	Cooking method
Root	Potatoes, sweet potatoes, yams, swedes, carrots, butternut squash, pumpkin	Boil and mash Roast Microwave
Traditional	Broccoli, cauliflower, green beans, cabbage, peas	Boil Steam Microwave
Mediterranean	Tomatoes, aubergine (eggplant), courgette (zucchini), red onion, mushroom, peppers	Roast Pan fry
Leafy Greens	Bok choy, pak choy, Chinese cabbage, spinach	Pan/stir fry Steam Microwave

As you can see, there are several different ways to cook vegetables, so you should be able to use one of the techniques below based on the cooking facilities available in your kitchen.

BOILING

This technique is good for cooking vegetables that you plan to mash, like potatoes and sweet potatoes. However, be mindful that a lot of other vegetables may lose some of their flavour when boiled. Half fill a saucepan with water and bring to the boil before adding your vegetables. Most vegetables will take about 5–10 minutes to cook through, so keep an eye on them and test with the tip of a sharp knife – if the knife cuts through to the centre easily, the vegetable is ready. Be careful not to overcook vegetables using this method as they will turn to mush very easily and lose their flavour and nutrients.

STEAMING

At home you may have a steamer, but it's unlikely this will be available in hostel kitchens. However, if you wish to steam your vegetables you can make your own steamer using a saucepan and a sieve. Fill about a quarter of the saucepan with water and bring to the boil. Place the sieve over the water (if the water touches the bottom of the sieve, take some out) and add your vegetables on top. Place the lid over the saucepan and cook until they are tender but still firm – this will depend on the type of vegetable and how big the pieces are. Make sure the water in the saucepan does not dry out.

ROASTING

This process takes the longest, but often produces the tastiest results. If you're roasting potatoes, always try to boil them first for 10 minutes to cut the overall cooking time down to around 30–40 minutes. Also try roasting Mediterranean vegetables (onions, tomatoes, peppers) on a moderate heat (180°C/350°F/gas mark 4) for 20 minutes.

PAN/STIR FRYING

This method has two dimensions to it. The first is for Mediterranean vegetables which are usually cooked in olive oil over a medium heat for 5–10 minutes until tender and caramelized. The other is for cooking leafy greens, usually in an Asian style, which involves using a little oil in a very hot frying pan and constantly moving the vegetable around for a couple of minutes.

MICROWAVING

The trick to cooking vegetables in the microwave is to ensure all of the pieces are cut into similar size chunks. Put them into a microwave-friendly container and cover with cling film. Pierce the film a couple of times to let steam escape and then put them in the microwave. They should take around 4–6 minutes for leafy vegetables, 8–10 minutes for traditional vegetables such as broccoli and beans, and 15 minutes for root vegetables.

Salad Dressings

BASIC VINAIGRETTE
6 tablespoons olive oil
2 tablespoons vinegar (balsamic, red wine, etc.)
Salt and pepper to taste

LEMON VINAIGRETTE
6 tablespoons olive oil
2 tablespoons lemon juice
Salt and pepper to taste

CREAMY DRESSING
½ cup mayonnaise
1 tablespoon lemon juice
1 tablespoon water
Salt and pepper to taste

Greek Salad

Serves 2

WHAT YOU'LL NEED:

Ingredients
1 small cucumber, diced
1 small red onion, diced
1 cup cherry tomatoes, halved
½ cup black olives
½ cup feta cheese, chopped into
   1.5 cm/⅔ in pieces
Dressing of your choice

Equipment
Bowl
Chopping board
Sharp knife
Cup

WHAT TO DO:
Combine all the ingredients in a bowl and mix thoroughly.

Pasta Salad

Serves 2

WHAT YOU'LL NEED:

Ingredients
200 g/7 oz pasta (e.g. shells, penne, spirals)
2 small tomatoes
1 clove garlic, crushed
1 small red onion, finely chopped
½ cup black or green olives (pitted)
¼ cup parsley or basil, finely chopped
Salt and pepper
Salad dressing of your choice

Equipment
Stove top
Large saucepan
Large bowl
Chopping board
Sharp knife

WHAT TO DO:

Cook the pasta in a large pan of boiling water according to packet instructions. When al dente, drain well and place in a bowl.

Cut the tomatoes in half, scoop out the seeds and cut the flesh into 1.5 cm/$^2/_3$ in dice. Add to the bowl along with the remaining ingredients while the pasta is still warm.

Stir well to combine and refrigerate before serving.

Note: For a more substantial meal you can add diced salami or leftover cooked chicken.

Potato Salad

Serves 2

WHAT YOU'LL NEED:

Ingredients	Equipment
4 medium potatoes (red skins look nice)	Stove top
	Large saucepan
2 eggs	Bowl
2 spring onions, chopped	Chopping board
¼ cup parsley, finely chopped	Sharp knife
Salt and pepper	Cup
Salad dressing of your choice	

WHAT TO DO:

Place the potatoes and eggs in a saucepan and cover with cold water. Bring to the boil and simmer gently for about 8 minutes.

Remove the eggs and refresh in cold water. Peel the eggs and chop into small pieces.

Continue cooking the potatoes until they are tender. Drain the potatoes and cut into 1.5 cm/$^2/_3$ in dice.

Combine all the ingredients in a bowl while the potatoes are still warm and mix thoroughly. Refrigerate before serving.

Note: For a more substantial meal you can add diced ham, precooked bacon or leftover cooked chicken.

Three Bean Salad

Serves 2

WHAT YOU'LL NEED:

Ingredients
400 g/14 oz can three bean
  mix, drained
1 small red onion, finely chopped
1 stalk of celery, finely chopped
1 small red pepper, finely chopped
1 clove garlic, crushed
Dressing of your choice

Equipment
Can opener
Chopping board
Sharp knife
Bowl

WHAT TO DO:
Combine all the ingredients in a bowl and mix thoroughly.

Tuna Nicoise Salad

Serves 2

WHAT YOU'LL NEED:

Ingredients	Equipment
1 cup new potatoes	Oven hob
1 egg	Saucepan
1 cup green beans	Chopping board
1 small lettuce	Sharp knife
1 tin tuna, drained	Bowl
Handful cherry tomatoes	

WHAT TO DO:

Fill the saucepan with water and bring to the boil. Add the potatoes and egg, and cook for 4–5 minutes.

Next add the green beans and cook for another 4 minutes. Drain the water out of the pan and set aside to cool.

Rinse the lettuce leaves and tear into bitesize pieces.

Shell the boiled egg and slice into quarters.

Assemble all the elements of the salad in a bowl and mix together.

Add the dressing of your choice and serve.

Cauliflower Cheese

Serves 2

WHAT YOU'LL NEED:

Ingredients	Equipment
½ small cauliflower	Stove top
125 ml/4 fl oz/½ cup milk	Oven
100 g/4 oz/1 cup (firmly packed)	Saucepan
cheddar cheese, grated	Shallow ovenproof dish
Salt and pepper	Small bowl
	Chopping board
	Sharp knife

WHAT TO DO:

Preheat the oven to 200°C/400°F/gas mark 6.

Cut the cauliflower into florets (small pieces). Cook the cauliflower in boiling water for about 3–4 minutes or until tender but still firm. Drain well and place in a shallow ovenproof dish.

Pour the milk into the saucepan and bring to the boil. Add the cheese (retaining 2 tablespoons) and seasoning and stir until melted and well combined.

Pour the cheese mixture over the cauliflower and sprinkle with the remaining cheese.

Bake the cauliflower cheese for 15 minutes or until the cheese is melted and golden brown on top.

Lentils with Peas and Bacon

Serves 2

WHAT YOU'LL NEED:

Ingredients
1 tablespoon olive oil
2 bacon rashers, chopped
1 cup peas (fresh or frozen)
400 g/14 oz can lentils,
    drained and rinsed
½ lemon, juiced
Handful fresh mint,
    chopped (optional)

Equipment
Stove top
Frying pan
Can opener
Chopping board
Sharp knife

WHAT TO DO:

Heat the oil in a frying pan and cook the bacon on a high heat until crisp.

Reduce the heat and add the peas. Put the lid on the frying pan and cook until the peas are tender (about 8 minutes for fresh peas, 5 minutes for frozen).

Add the lentils and cook until warmed through. Remove from the heat and add the lemon juice and a drizzle of oil.

Just before serving, stir through the fresh mint.

Ratatouille

Serves 2

WHAT YOU'LL NEED:

Ingredients
1 red pepper
1 small aubergine/eggplant
1 medium courgette/zucchini
3 tomatoes
1 small onion
2 tablespoons oil
1 clove garlic, finely chopped
½ tablespoon dried Italian herbs
Salt and pepper

Equipment
Stove top
Saucepan
Chopping board
Sharp knife
Tablespoon

WHAT TO DO:
Cut all the vegetables into 1.5 cm/²/₃ in dice.

Heat the oil in a saucepan, add the onion and cook for about 5 minutes until softened.

Add the other vegetables and remaining ingredients and simmer for about 15 minutes or until the vegetables are tender.

Rice and Potato Cakes

Serves 2

WHAT YOU'LL NEED:

Ingredients	Equipment
1 large potato, peeled and quartered	Stove top
110 g/4 oz/½ cup medium grain rice	Large saucepan
1 egg, lightly beaten	Frying pan
25 g/1 oz/¼ cup parmesan	Bowl
cheese, grated	Grater
1 clove garlic, crushed	Cup
Salt and pepper	
Oil for frying	

WHAT TO DO:

Place the potato in a large saucepan and pour in enough water to cover. Bring to the boil and cook the potato until tender. Drain, mash until smooth and set aside to cool.

Refill the saucepan with water and bring to the boil. Add the rice and cook for about 12 minutes or until tender. Drain and set aside to cool.

In a bowl, combine the rice, mashed potato, egg, cheese, garlic and seasoning and mix well.

Divide the mixture into 4 balls and flatten into patties. Refrigerate for ½ hour if you have time.

Heat the oil in a frying pan over a medium heat. Add the rice and potato cakes and cook for about 5 minutes on each side.

Stir-fried Asian Greens

Serves 2

WHAT YOU'LL NEED:

Ingredients
1 tablespoon olive oil
1 clove garlic, crushed
2 cm/¾ in piece fresh ginger, thinly sliced
1 cup mixed greens (pak choi, bok choy, Chinese cabbage, spring onions, broccoli)
2 tablespoons water
1 tablespoon sesame oil (optional)
1 tablespoon soy sauce

Equipment
Stove top
Frying pan
Chopping board
Sharp knife
Tablespoon

WHAT TO DO:

Heat the olive oil in a frying pan (or wok if available) and add the garlic and ginger. Cook for 1–2 minutes until the garlic changes colour.

Add the mixed greens and toss for about 2 minutes. Add the water and place the lid on the pan. Cook for 2–3 minutes until the vegetables are tender but still firm.

Add the sesame oil and soy sauce and serve.

Desserts

Fruit Crumble see page 137

Baked Chocolate Bananas

Serves 2

WHAT YOU'LL NEED:

Ingredients
2 bananas
100 g/4 oz dark chocolate

Equipment
Oven
Sharp knife
Aluminium foil

WHAT TO DO:

Preheat the oven to 180°C/350°F/gas mark 4.

Using a sharp knife, make a slit along one side of the bananas, making sure you don't cut through the skin on the opposite side.

Break the chocolate into chunks and insert into the slits.
Wrap each banana in a piece of foil.

Bake the bananas for about 10 minutes or until the chocolate has melted. Remove the bananas from the foil and serve with ice cream or cream.

Chocolate Velvet Cups

Serves 2

WHAT YOU'LL NEED:

Ingredients
65 ml/2 fl oz/¼ cup milk
1 cup white marshmallows
100 g/4 oz dark chocolate,
  broken into pieces
250 ml/8 fl oz/1 cup thick cream

Equipment
Stove top
Saucepan
Cup

WHAT TO DO:

Pour the milk into a saucepan and add the marshmallows and
chocolate pieces. Cook over a very gentle heat stirring all the time
to ensure chocolate does not burn on the bottom of the pan.
When the mixture has melted remove from the heat and allow
to cool for 5–10 minutes.

Add the cream (reserving 2 blobs for serving) and stir to combine.
Pour the chocolate mixture into coffee cups and refrigerate for at
least an hour. Top with blobs of cream before serving.

Creamy Pears

Serves 2

WHAT YOU'LL NEED:

Ingredients	Equipment
2 pears	Oven
$2/3$ cup cream	Ovenproof dish
1 tablespoon sugar	Small bowl
2 tablespoons ground almonds	Chopping board
	Sharp knife
	Tablespoon

WHAT TO DO:

Preheat the oven to 180°C/350°F/gas mark 4.

Peel the pears, cut into halves and remove the cores.
Place cut-side down in an ovenproof dish.

Place the cream, sugar and almonds in a bowl and stir well
to combine. Pour the mixture over the pears.

Bake the pears for 20–30 minutes. May be served hot or cold.

Eton Mess

Serves 2

WHAT YOU'LL NEED:

Ingredients
1 cup fresh strawberries
2 tablespoons sugar
4 meringues
250 ml/8 fl oz/1 cup thick cream

Equipment
Bowl
Chopping board
Sharp knife

WHAT TO DO:
Hull the strawberries by removing the green stalk and leaves,
then chop into quarters.

Toss the strawberries in the sugar and set aside for as long as possible.

Crumble the meringues into bitesize pieces.

In a bowl, combine the cream, crumbled meringues, strawberries
and the juice that will have developed. Mix gently and serve.

French Toast with Caramelized Banana

Serves 2

WHAT YOU'LL NEED:

Ingredients	Equipment
2 eggs	Stove top
125 ml/4 fl oz/½ cup milk	Frying pan
2 slices bread (2 cm/¾ in thick)	Shallow bowl
4 tablespoons butter	Chopping board
2 tablespoons sugar	Sharp knife
2 small bananas	Tablespoon
	Cup

WHAT TO DO:

Whisk the eggs and milk in a shallow bowl. Place the slices of bread in the bowl and allow them to soak up the egg mixture. Turn the bread over and leave until most of the liquid has been absorbed into the bread.

Put half the butter in a frying pan and melt over a medium–low heat. Add the bread and cook on both sides until golden brown. Transfer to a plate and keep warm.

Melt the remaining butter in the frying pan, add the sugar and stir until dissolved.

Cut the bananas into 2 cm/¾ in slices (on an angle) and place in the butter. Cook the banana, stirring, for about 4–5 minutes until golden brown.

Serve toast topped with caramelized banana.

Fruit Crumble

Serves 2

WHAT YOU'LL NEED:

Ingredients	Equipment
1 cup fresh fruit (e.g. apples, berries, peaches, pears)	Stove top
	Saucepan
2 tablespoons sugar	Bowl
2 tablespoons water	Chopping board
6 plain biscuits (e.g. digestives, hobnobs, ginger nuts)	Sharp knife

WHAT TO DO:

Prepare the fruit by peeling, de-seeding and roughly chopping.

Place the fruit in a saucepan along with the sugar and water and cook over a low heat for 10 minutes (depending on the fruit).

Remove the fruit from the heat and place into serving bowls. Crush the biscuits and sprinkle over the top of the cooked fruit.

Lemon Creams

Serves 2

WHAT YOU'LL NEED:

Ingredients	Equipment
250 ml/8 fl oz/1 cup thick cream	Stove top
½ cup sugar	Saucepan
1 lemon (zest and juice)	Grater
	Cup

WHAT TO DO:

Place the cream and sugar in a saucepan over a low heat and slowly bring to the boil. Simmer for about 3 minutes then remove from the heat and allow to cool.

Add the lemon juice and zest and whisk well.

Pour the mixture into two glasses and refrigerate for 2–3 hours until the lemon cream sets.

Pancakes

Serves 2

WHAT YOU'LL NEED:

Ingredients	Equipment
125 g/4½ oz/1 cup flour	Stove top
250 ml/8 fl oz/1 cup milk	Frying pan (preferably non-stick)
1 egg, beaten	Bowl
1 tablespoon oil	Tablespoon
Topping of your choice	Cup
(e.g. sugar and lemon,	
chocolate spread, jam)	

WHAT TO DO:

Combine the flour, milk and egg in a bowl and mix thoroughly to ensure there are no lumps.

Heat a little oil in the frying pan and add a quarter of the mixture. Swirl the frying pan around until the mixture has covered the base of the pan. When the pancake starts to bubble flip it over and cook on the other side. Remove from the frying pan and serve with the topping of your choice. Repeat to make 3 more pancakes.

Rice Pudding

Serves 2

WHAT YOU'LL NEED:

Ingredients	Equipment
310 ml/10 fl oz/1¼ cups milk	Stove top
2 tablespoons sugar	Saucepan with lid
85 g/3 oz/⅓ cup short grain rice	Cup
125 ml/4 fl oz/½ cup cream	Tablespoon

WHAT TO DO:

Pour the milk into a saucepan and bring to the boil over a medium heat.

Add the sugar and rice and stir the mixture while bringing back to the boil.

Put a lid on the saucepan and simmer over a very gentle heat, stirring frequently, for about 35 minutes until the rice is tender.

Add the cream and cook for a further 5 minutes until the rice is thick and creamy.

Note: For additional flavour you could add lemon/orange zest, honey or raisins.

Warm Chocolate Dip

Serves 2

WHAT YOU'LL NEED:

Ingredients	Equipment
85 ml/3 fl oz/⅓ cup cream	Stove top
125 g/4½ oz dark chocolate,	Saucepan
broken into pieces	Bowl
	Cup

WHAT TO DO:

Pour the cream into a saucepan and slowly heat until nearly boiling. Remove from the heat, add the chocolate and stir until it has melted and is smooth.

Transfer to a bowl and serve with your choice of fresh strawberries, sliced bananas, orange segments, marshmallows or biscuits.

Glossary

Al dente: Italian term used to describe pasta that is cooked until tender but still has a firm, chewy texture.

Bake: To cook in the oven.

Beat: To vigorously stir ingredients with a spoon or whisk to make a smooth mixture.

Blend: To add ingredients together and stir with a spoon.

Boil: To heat a liquid until bubbles break continually on the surface.

Brown: To cook meat or vegetables in a pan with oil or butter over a high heat until they turn brown in colour.

Caramelize: To cook meat or vegetables in a pan with oil or butter over a high heat until it turns brown in colour. (A small amount of sugar can be added to the pan to assist the process.)

Chop: To cut solid food into pieces with a sharp knife.

Combine: To add ingredients together.

Crush: To squash food into tiny pieces with a heavy utensil, e.g. rolling pin or kitchen mallet.

Drizzle: To pour a liquid over food in a slow, light trickle.

Fillet: A piece of meat, chicken or fish after the bone has been removed.

Fry: To cook food in hot oil or butter.

Grate: To rub food on a grater to shred into tiny pieces.

Grease: To rub a pan with oil or butter to stop food from sticking when cooked.

Grill: To cook food under an intense heat source.

Marinate: To add flavour to food prior to cooking by placing it in a mixture of liquid and seasoning/spice (marinade).

Mash: To press food with a masher or fork to remove lumps.

Peel: To remove the outer peel from vegetables or fruits.

Pinch: A very small amount of food (usually seasoning or spice) that you can hold between your thumb and forefinger.

Reduce: To boil liquid down to reduce the volume, thicken and intensify the flavour.

Sauté: To cook and/or brown food in a small amount of hot oil or butter.

Simmer: To cook over a low heat so the liquid doesn't reach boiling point but gentle bubbles slowly break the surface.

Stir-fry: To cook food (usually cut into strips) on a high heat with a small amount of oil while stirring constantly.

Whip/Whisk: To mix together by beating rapidly with a fork or whisk.

Zest: To finely grate the outer skin of citrus fruits.

Conversions

OVEN CONVERSIONS

Degrees Celsius	Degrees Fahrenheit	Gas Mark
110	225	¼
130	250	½
140	275	1
150	300	2
170	325	3
180	350	4
190	375	5
200	400	6
220	425	7
230	450	8
240	475	9

LIQUID CONVERSIONS

Metric	Imperial	Cups
30 ml	1 fl oz	⅛ cup
60 ml	2 fl oz	¼ cup
80 ml	2¾ fl oz	⅓ cup
125 ml	4 fl oz	½ cup
185 ml	6 fl oz	¾ cup
250 ml	8 fl oz	1 cup

MEASUREMENT CONVERSIONS

Metric	Imperial
1 cm	0.4 in
1.5 cm	0.6 in
2 cm	0.8 in
2.5 cm	1 in
3 cm	1.2 in
3.5 cm	1.4 in
4 cm	1.6 in
4.5 cm	1.8 in
5 cm	2 in

Notes

Notes

Recipe Index

SNACKS AND SOUPS. 23
Bruschetta. 24
Chorizo and Beans. 25
Flatbread Pizza with Rosemary and Garlic 26
Guacamole 27
Mexican Scrambled Eggs 28
Nachos 29
Omelette. 30
Pizza Subs 31
Potato Wedges 32
Bean and Tomato Soup 33
Chicken Noodle Soup. 34
Corn Chowder 35
Crushed Pea and Mint Soup. 36
French Onion Soup 37
Mushroom Soup 38

CHICKEN DISHES 39
Baked Chicken and Mushrooms 41
Baked Chicken with Green Olives 42
Chicken and Bacon Burgers 43
Chicken Cacciatore 44
Chicken Curry. 45
Chicken Fajitas 46
Chicken Parmigiana 47

Chicken Quesadillas 48
Chicken and Vegetable Stack 49
Chicken Wings with Lime and Chilli 50
Chicken Wrapped in Prosciutto 51
Chilli Chicken Stir-fry 52
Creamy Chicken and Spinach 53
Parmesan Drumsticks 54
Sticky Chicken Wings 55

MEAT DISHES 56
Chorizo and Chickpea Stew 59
Beef Stroganoff 60
Chilli Con Carne 61
Chow Mein 62
Cottage Pie 63
Garlic Beef Stir-fry 64
Hamburgers 65
Mince and Cabbage Bake 66
Sausage Casserole 67
Savoury Mince 68
Greek Lamb Chops 69
Lamb and Feta Patties 70
Pork Chops with Cider Sauce 71
Moussaka 72
Pork with Mushrooms and Wine 74

FISH DISHES 75
Baked Fish and Asparagus Parcels 77
Baked Fish with Tomato and Thyme 78
Baked Salmon and Crushed Peas 79
Fish Cakes 80
Fish Stew 81
Poached Salmon Fillets 82

Salmon and Corn Bake 83
Tuna Slice 84
Creole Prawns. 85
Garlic and Lemon Prawns 86

PASTA AND RICE DISHES 87
Macaroni Cheese 90
Pasta Aglio e Olio (Garlic and Olive Oil) 91
Pasta Bolognaise. 92
Pasta Carbonara 93
Pasta Puttanesca. 94
Pasta with Lemon and Basil 95
Pasta with Salami and Mushrooms 96
Pasta with Tuna and Tomatoes. 97
Spaghetti with Meatballs 98
Budget Paella 99
Fried Rice. 100
Kedgeree 101
Moroccan Rice 102
Thai Chicken Coconut Rice 103
Risotto 104

VEGETARIAN DISHES 106
Baked Mushrooms. 107
Bubble and Squeak Patties. 108
Couscous and Roasted Vegetables 109
Frittata 110
Spicy Dahl 111
Spinach and Mushroom Soufflé Omelette 112
Tofu Provencal 113
Vegetarian Moussaka. 114
Courgette/zucchini Fritters 115
Spanish Baked Eggs 116

SALADS AND VEGETABLES 117
Salad Dressings. 120
Greek Salad 121
Pasta Salad. 122
Potato Salad. 123
Three Bean Salad. 124
Tuna Nicoise Salad. 125
Cauliflower Cheese 126
Lentils with Peas and Bacon. 127
Ratatouille 128
Rice and Potato Cakes 129
Stir-fried Asian Greens 130

DESSERTS. 131
Baked Chocolate Bananas. 132
Chocolate Velvet Cups 133
Creamy Pears 134
Eton Mess 135
French Toast with Caramelized Banana 136
Fruit Crumble 137
Lemon Creams 138
Pancakes 139
Rice Pudding. 140
Warm Chocolate Dip 141

Chicken Wings with Lime and Chilli see *page 50*